The Greatest Amateur In The World

By Peter McDougall

Cover: The American team captain, Bobby Jones, congratulates E. J. (Ted) McDougall at the completion of his third round, St Andrews, October 1958.

ISBN:1530973155
ISBN-13:9781530973156

DEDICATION

This book is dedicated to Leonie Kathleen Pikett. She first meet Edward when she was seventeen years of age and they married when she was the youthful age of nineteen. Leonie kept an extensive scrap book of Edward's achievements from as early as 1955. There are literally thousands of newspaper clippings kept in a number of scrap books. Leonie passed away aged 66 years peacefully at home surrounded by family at Mangawhai Heads.

CONTENTS

Scottish Midland Boys Champion - 1951

ACKNOWLEDGMENTS

Ted McDougall played alongside some of the great golfers of all time including Sam Snead, Gary Player, Peter Thomson, Nick Faldo, Billy Casper, Tony Jacklin, Lanny Wadkins, Kel Nagle, Bob Charles, and Marilynn Smith from US LPGA tour.

Ted played in seven World Amateur Team Championship played for the Eisenhower Trophy. The approach taken in writing this book is to link in a logical manner the more interesting articles written by some of the best local and foreign correspondents and tell Ted's through their eyes. The journalists included Fred Tupper - special correspondent to the New York Times, T. P. McLean from the New Zealand Herald, Jim Wallace, Winston Hooper, Ian Wells, Owen Cooke, Alan Graham, Brian Doherty, J. A. Gasparich, and two who went by the pseudonyms R.E.M. and the Nineteenth. Permission has been granted from NZME Publishing Ltd to re-print extracts from these newspaper articles. Contributions from Stephen Carruthers of the Pitlochry Golf Club, Ian Panton of Edinburgh, Gavin Cortesi of the Tokoroa Golf Club, Ian Litchfield of the Pukekohe Golf Club and Karen Osborne from the Peninsula Golf Club have assisted me in filling in any missing gaps. Valuable information has also been obtained from the Monifieth Golf Club Centenary Booklet 1858-1958, and the Waikato Golf Association Celebrates its First Fifty Years 1947-1997 booklet.

1 NEW ZEALAND AMATEUR CHAMPION

When twenty year old Edward John McDougall from the Pukekohe Golf Club in South Auckland won the 1957 New Zealand Amateur played on the Hokowhitu golf course in Palmerston North, beating W.W. (Bill) Smith from the Titirangi club in Auckland in the final, it should not have come as a surprise to anyone.

In the 1955 New Zealand Open, held at the Middlemore course in Auckland, the then eighteen year old McDougall scored a two under par 70 in the second round with his headmaster Dan Bryant from Pukekohe High School as his caddy. His round of 70 was the lowest score of the first thirty six holes of the tournament.

In 1956, his first year out of school, Ted won his first of three consecutive Stewart Gold Cups held each year in September at the Grange Golf Club in Auckland. The Stewart Gold Cup along with the Auckland Stroke Play are Auckland's premier stroke play events.

His win was reported in the NZ Herald as follows;

Five strokes ahead of the rest of the field, the 19-year-old Pukekohe golfer E. McDougall took the Grange club's 72-hole Stewart Gold Cup with a total of 291 yesterday.

His final round was a spanking 69, which equaled the course record. The runner-up was D. L. Woon, of Hamilton, the former holder of the trophy, who also recorded a 69.

A well-built young man, McDougall not only towered above his opponents in stature, but *also in the quality of his play. The sole `exception was Woon, who made a brilliant recovery with a final round of 69 to pull up from well behind after the first 36 holes.*

Results: Stewart Gold Cup - September 1956 - Grange Golf Club

1	**E. McDougall (Pukekohe)**	**72**	**76**	**74**	**69**	**291**
2	D. L. Woon (Hamilton)	80	74	73	69	296
3	G. Adams	71	77	73	76	297
4	F. Cullen (Matamata)	76	72	75	76	299
5	W. W. Smith	77	74	72	77	300
6	N. V. Edwards	75	77	75	75	302
7=	K. McFarlane (Putaruru)	81	73	81	70	305
7=	R. Newdick	80	72	76	77	305
9	I Dyer	79	75	76	77	307
10	M. Szigetvary	76	73	82	78	309

That same year he also won the Northland Match Play Championship beating A. C. Aplin from Whangarei 2 and 1 in the final on the Mt Denby golf course.

Despite McDougall's good form in 1956 he was overlooked for selection for the Auckland six man team to contest the national interprovincial tournament. He had missed a good part of the competitive season when the New Zealand Government required him to attend the Papakura Military Camp.

Under the Military Training Act 1949 all males became liable for military service upon reaching 18 years of age. They had to undergo fourteen weeks of intensive full time training. This was changed in 1961 to a ballot based system upon reaching the age of 20.

In January 1957 Ted played in the Tauranga Invitational tournament. This tournament was part of quite an extensive New Zealand professional circuit that existed at the time. Leading New Zealand amateurs were also invited to play.

E. J. McDougall, the man who could not win a place in the Auckland Freyberg Rose Bowl team, yesterday demonstrated both his class and promise by easily winning the annual Tauranga invitation golf tournament. He finished five strokes ahead of R. R. Newdick, the second amateur, and six strokes ahead of E. A. Southerden, the first professional. Professional prizes totaled £150.

Results: 5TH Tauranga Invitation Tournament - January 1957

1	**E. J. McDougall* (Pukekohe)**	**73**	**71**	**67**	**211**
2	R. R. Newdick* (North Shore)	75	69	72	216
3	E. A. Southerden (Napier)	75	70	72	217
4	F. X. Buckler (Hamilton)	72	73	73	218
5=	A. E. Guy (Auckland)	73	77	70	220
5=	R. A. Jackson (Auckland)	70	77	73	220
7	F. J. Cullen* (Matamata)	73	71	77	221
8=	S. G. Jones* (Hastings)	81	72	70	223
8=	I. E. Deadman* (Rotorua)	75	69	79	223
10	R. H. Glading* (Hamilton)	79	75	70	224

*Denotes amateur

The Pukekohe Golf Club was a member of the Franklin Sub Association of Auckland. The Sub Association, for the first time, entered a team into the Auckland 'A' Grade Pennant series. They had considerable success.

In April in the first round Franklin defeated Remuera 6 ½ games to 5 ½ games. McDougall beat Fenton 3 and 2 in the morning and Randrup 2 and 1 in the afternoon.

On June the 10th they defeated Manukau 7 ½ to 4 ½ with McDougall defeating N. Dyer 5 and 4 and R. Harsant 4 and 3. This match was played at the Grange Golf Club. - *MacDougall at last was placing his whole 16 stone 5 pounds in the right place at the right time and many of his tee shots were phenomenal in length and accuracy. At the 13th, for instance, a long 480-yard, bogey 5 hole, MacDougall in his morning round, hit a colossal drive into a stiff wind and then gently tapped a five iron through the green. Most other players were more than pleased to see two hearty woods getting close to the front of the green.*

On June 24 Franklin defeated Titirangi 6 ½ games to 5 ½ games with McDougall completing wins against N. Edwards 5 and 3 and W.W. Smith 3 and 2.

Despite this success McDougall was again overlooked for selection for the Auckland team to compete for the Freyberg Rose Bowl.

The Special Correspondent for the NZ Herald would report … *MacDougall even expressed a singularly stern and wild Caledonia by winning practically everything in sight round the Auckland province however because of an indifferent round in the qualifying competition of the Auckland Easter Championship, he was incontinently dropped from the Freyberg Rose Bowl Team.*

In September that year he successfully defended the Stewart Gold Cup.

…although he lapsed badly at one stage to record a nine for a par-4 hole, he made up for it by a number of birdies that stood to him in the end.

Results: Stewart Gold Cup - September 1957 - Grange Golf Club

1	**E. J. McDougall (Pukekohe)**	71	75	77	72	295
2	I Dawson (Kaikohe)	74	72	75	75	296
3	N. V. Edwards (Titirangi)	75	73	73	79	300
4	J. C. Oliver (Titirangi)	74	75	77	75	301
5	M. Szigetvary (Pupuke)	77	72	76	78	303
6=	I. W Dyer.	72	79	77	78	306
6=	R. R. Newdick (N. Shore)	74	73	76	83	306
8=	G. R. Adams (Grange)	77	80	75	77	309

8=	W. W. Smith (Titirangi)	78	78	77	76	309
10	J. Boon (Grange)	77	71	82	82	312

Although McDougall had successfully defended the Stewart Golf Cup his immediate form leading into the NZ Amateur had not been encouraging having performed poorly in a warm up event held at the Hutt Club in Wellington.

He therefore went into the 1957 NZ Amateur, played in October, with low expectations. That all changed however when with great encouragement from his fellow protégée and good friend Ross Newdick they combined to win the New Zealand foursomes title.

Prior to 1964 the NZ Amateur and the NZ Open were a combined event. At the completion of the 72-holes the field was split with the leading 64 amateurs playing a match play event to determine the amateur champion.

The leading professionals also continued on to determine their match play champion.

In this particular year Bob Charles was third equal overall in the NZ Open and the leading amateur and therefore he top-qualified for the amateur side of the match play.

McDougall was tenth equal overall and qualified for the match play as fifth amateur.

The Australian Kel Nagle was for the first time the overall NZ Open champion, ahead of Peter Thomson, and the top qualifier for the professional division.

The *Golf reporter* wrote on the match play under the headline - SMITH SHOWS FINE FORM WITH PUTTER IN AMATEUR GOLF

PALMERSTON NORTH, Wednesday. - Two Aucklanders, Bill Smith (Titirangi) and Ted McDougall (Pukekohe) yesterday reached the semi-finals of the New Zealand amateur golf championship at Hokowhitu, Palmerston North.

In the quarter-finals Smith beat his club mate Neil Edwards 4 and 3 and McDougall beat the 1955 champion Stuart Jones, 3 and 2.

Semi-final draw: Smith v. Jack Lacy (New Plymouth), McDougall v. Ian Harvey (Christchurch)

Auckland provincial champion Smith struck true form for the first time against Edwards, especially on and around the greens. He reached the turn two under scratch and was still one under when the match finished.

Edwards, who earlier played the role of giant-killer by beating Bob Charles (Christchurch) and Ross Newdick (North Shore), said after the match: "He was tremendous with his putter. Either the ball fell in the hole or stopped right on the lip from any distance."

Twenty year old McDougall successfully turned on his full power for the first time. Onlookers gasped as tee shots sped down the fairway almost out of sight.

A couple of times, McDougall was seen playing delightful recoveries from a couple of fairways off the beaten track.

But it made little difference. He was on top of the world and in the mood to win, and in that frame of mind is practically invincible.

In the morning, McDougall polished off Ken Carter (Miramar) 4 and 3 after reaching the turn in 33, four under scratch. Against Jones, although not quite so brilliant, he was always on top and ended the match in irrepressible style with two birdies.

The putt which won the match- a 30 footer on the 16th-had even McDougall gazing in wonder. The ball was struck firmly but obviously a foot or two off line.

Suddenly the ball hit an old pitch mark, jumped four inches into the air, and headed off straight into the hole.

Smith, greatly pleased to reach the semi-finals, said that he felt like a grandfather when he considered the age of the other three semi-finalists. McDougall and Harvey are both 20 and Lacy in his middle 20s. Smith gave his age as somewhere in the 40s.

Mystery man

Lacy has been round Hokowhitu like some sort of mystery man-seen but rarely noticed. Not until he won his quarter-final against former Universities champion Pete Carver did people start asking: "Who is this bloke? We've never heard of him."

Apparently Lacy is recognized in New Plymouth as a steady match player. An architect-builder, Lacy played sixth for Taranaki at the Freyberg Rose Bowl tournament at Gisborne earlier this year, winning five of his matches.

Stockily built, he has a reputation for a grand temperament and is not upset to any great extent by inclement weather.

Tourney stylist

Slightly built Harvey, who represented Canterbury in the Rose Bowl tournament, is the stylist of the tournament and gets an extraordinary amount of length off the tees. In the morning he beat Waikato hitter Tim Woon 1 up and outdrove Woon at nearly every hole.

In the afternoon he made Brian Silk (Wanganui) look as if he was using an iron. Harvey beat an unusually inaccurate Silk 3 and 2.

McDougall would encounter a torrid time in the semi-final against the 20 year old Ian Harvey from the Waitikiri club in Christchurch.

The *Golf reporter* would write on the semi-final matches under the headline; AUCKLAND GOLFERS MAKE HISTORY IN N.Z. TOURNAMENT.

PALMERSTON NORTH, Thursday.-Two Scottish-born Aucklanders, Bill Smith (Titirangi) and Ted McDougall (Pukekohe) are today making history in the final of the New Zealand golf championship at the Hokowhitu course here.

It is the first time that two Aucklanders have played off for the title. Not since Pax Smith won at Balmacewan in 1938 has an Auckland player been in the final.

In the semi-finals yesterday Smith beat Jack Lacy 7 and 6 and McDougall beat Ian Harvey (Waitikiri) one up.

......Harvey took the lead when McDougall failed with a four footer at the 28th after his second to the green was wide. At the deceptive 31st (13th) a birdie three gave Harvey what looked like an unassailable lead.

Then for the first time McDougall unleashed his powerful shoulders and birdies at the 32nd (14th) and the 33rd, (15th) both par fives, once more brought the match square.

The 35th (17th) was the deciding hole. Both were through the green with their seconds.

Harvey chipped back 10 feet from the flag and McDougall putted dead.

After much deliberation, Harvey stabbed the ball short of the hole and McDougall smiled for the first time as he dropped his 12 inches for the win.

Once news had reached Pukekohe that McDougall had reached the final, a contingent including his father and former headmaster Mr. Bryant decided to make the journey by overnight train to Palmerston North.

Encouraged by this support and with his best friend from high school Dave Adams caddying for him he went into the final in a very confident mood.

The final however was some-what of an anti-climax as Smith, who was a very accomplished Auckland golfer, *appeared nervous in the final and was unsettled by McDougall's relaxed approach.* McDougall was now playing the golf of his life and went to lunch 4up. Smith's struggles continued in the afternoon and he eventually went down 5 and 4.

On the professional side of the draw Kel Nagle overcame one of New Zealand's finest professional golfers in the form of Alex Murray to win the professional final 1up.

Welcome the new champion - arrangements were to be made for the New Zealand amateur champion golfer, E.J. 'Ted' MacDougall, to be welcomed when he steps from the Limited express, at Pukekohe Railway Station at about 8.20 a.m. tomorrow. He will be accorded a Civic welcome by the Mayor, Mr. S. C. Childs, and councilors outside the Pukekohe Post Office at 8.30.

The president, Dr. W. B. Allen, and executive of the Pukekohe Golf Club, will be the hosts at a welcome social evening to Ted MacDougall, in the golf house tomorrow night at eight o'clock. Members of the Auckland Golf association, and the Franklin sub association are expected to be present to join in congratulating the new champion. All members of the club and their friends are invited to be present. The ladies are asked to take a plate of something to eat.

Ted's father Eddie made a gracious thank you speech on behalf of his family. Eddie McDougall had moved his family from Moulin, a small village on the outskirts of Pitlochry, Scotland to New Zealand in 1952 to begin a new life.

They had also considered the United States where Eddie's wife Jane had an older brother and sister living but instead settled for Pukekohe where she also had a brother, Gordon, and sister, Margaret, living close by.

To understand why so many Scots left their homeland during this period can be explained by a recent article written by Chris McCall in the Scotsman under the headline - **The Scottish diaspora: How Scots spread across the Globe:**

The phrase refers to the vast number of people around the world who wish to retain a connection to Scotland. The tradition of Scots moving, for a variety of reasons, to south of the border or further afield dates back more than eight centuries.

A significant proportion of people born in Scotland - at least 20 per cent - live elsewhere in the UK or overseas, according to a 2009 Scottish Government report. Scots are also more likely to leave their homeland and settle elsewhere than any other English-speaking peoples. Around 19 per cent of Irish people live outside of Ireland, followed by 14 per cent of New Zealanders. The figure for the US, Canada and South Africa is 5.6 per cent or less

Following England, the next most popular destinations for the Scots diaspora is Australia, the US, Canada, New Zealand and Wales.

At the height of the industrial revolution in the late 18th and early 19th centuries immigration was a fact of life for many Scots. But while the infamous clearances led to many Highland and island communities being forcefully dispersed by landowners, there were thousands more who voluntarily chose to leave their homeland and were grateful for the opportunity to do so.

Research by Prof Devine and others has found much of the diaspora are descendants of lowland Scots who decided to make a better life abroad - and not "Gaels thrown off their land".

'The immensely popular books of 'victim history' by the Canadian writer, John Prebble in the 1960s and 1970s, on such themes as Culloden and the clearances, have helped to forge the myth of Scottish emigration as a Highland experience, a diaspora of the clans" Prof Devine told the Scotsman in 2009.

It remains a belief shared by many Scots and overwhelmingly so by the Scottish diaspora in North America today who base their 'history' of the nation on Prebble and similar authors and remain quite unaware of the huge advances in the transformed understanding of Scotland's complex past made over the past few decades.

During WWII Eddie McDougall was based in Cambridge, England with the R. A. F. He was involved in communications during the war and his family were able to live close by. Edward as a seven year old attended Shrubbery School in Cambridge.

At the end of WWII the family returned to Pitlochry and Edward as a young lad started caddying to earn a few extra shillings. He soon developed more than a passing interest in the game and started playing golf himself. His father was a member of the club and played to a 12 handicap. The Professional at Pitlochry at the time was Johnny Murray and John Panton was briefly his assistant.

John Panton had completed his apprenticeship with John Letters in Glasgow in the late 1930's and he also worked for David Lows as a coach in Dundee. He then served Britain in WWII. After the war he was 'debunked' and spent a summer at Pitlochry before taking up the role as professional at the Glenbervie Golf Club in 1948.

John Panton would become a legend of the game in Scotland. He played on three Ryder Cup teams and was honorary professional of the Royal and Ancient Golf Club St Andrews from 1988 until his retirement in 2006.

Edward would have been influenced by John Panton but more so by Johnny Murray. Edward was essentially self-taught on the fundamentals of the golf swing which were engrained at a very young age. He learnt the game by observing the likes of John Panton and Johnny Murray. Edward would also follow his father, who on a Sunday afternoon, played in a 'big match' with Ian Panton, Geordie Mitchell and Jock Grant.

Ian Panton was a scratch player and it was Ian, the brother of John, who would have the biggest influence on the development of Edward's game.

No-one could afford to pay for golf lessons immediately after the war and Edward would never have a formal golf lesson in his life other than tinkering with the odd tip he received now and then but only if he felt it absolutely necessary.

In the summer holidays Edward would often play three rounds of golf in one day. Pitlochry had some very good junior golfers at the time and Ted would have some keen competition from players like John Brydone and Sandy "Baldy" Scott.

Edward was Pitlochry school champion in 1950 and 1951 and at the age of fourteen he won the Scottish Midlands boys championship at the North Inch golf course. King James VI played on Perth's North Inch Golf Course in the 1500s and it is one the first recognizable golf courses in the world, alongside Musselburgh, that is still in play today.

After arriving from Scotland at the age of 14 Edward quickly settled into life as a student at Pukekohe High School and he would become life-long friends with David Adams. They were both prefects of the school. David was a very good middle distance runner. They also played for the first fifteen rugby team. Edward was already a big athletic lad and was rated highly as a number eight. Had he not been so good at golf he may have considered taking rugby further.

The Pukekohe High headmaster "Dynamic Dan" Bryant, as he liked to be referred to as, was a major influence on Edward's early life in New Zealand. - *A man of enormous enthusiasm, energy and a sense of purpose and extremely hard working he would be a major inspiration for his students and indeed most people that he would come into contact with. - The Bryant Era - Pukekohe High School*

Mr. Bryant had been influential in both mountaineering and rugby. Tragically he was killed in a motor vehicle accident not long after watching his former pupil win the New Zealand Amateur

After leaving school, having gone right through the grades to 7th form, Edward started out on his career as a bank clerk for the Bank of New Zealand at their Pukekohe branch. He still lived at home with his parents and younger sister Margaret.

In early 1958 at the conclusion of the Auckland trials played in February and March the following Auckland team was selected; Ted McDougall at No. 1 followed by Ross Newdick, Bill Smith, Neil Edwards, Jack Oliver and Neville Dowden to compete in the national interprovincial tournament.

The interprovincial tournament is played amongst the twelve associations represented on the New Zealand Golf Council. It is played over six rounds of match play in May each year.

They competed for the Freyberg Rose Bowl. The inaugural tournament commenced in 1951 and in the early years was dominated by Manawatu-Wanganui winning the event four years in a row from 1952. Wellington and Canterbury had also won the event. Auckland had yet to register a win.

The Auckland team arrived at the Tahunanui course in Nelson four days early and had five practice rounds prior to the start of the tournament. This intense preparation paid off as they went through the six rounds of match play undefeated to claim their maiden victory.

MacDougall came out of the tournament extremely well and by beating S. G. Jones and J. D. Durry, both who seem to be on everybody's list for the World Tournament at St Andrews in October, he must almost certainly have established a right to the team. At this juncture, incidentally, I should be much inclined to say that Jones, MacDougall, and R. J. Charles must be in the team and that there will be keenest of competition for the final place among Silk, Durry and Newdick. - Nineteenth.

By early 1958 the United States Golf Association (USGA) had received several invitations to host an international team event. The USGA respond by sending a delegation to Scotland to meet with the Royal and Ancient society for discussions on a possible international event. The idea is well received and The World Amateur Golf Council was formed in May with 32 member countries.

The first World Amateur Teams event is to be played at St Andrews in October. The *Friends of American Golf* were to play an instrumental part in making all this happen and are honored at a function at the White House by President Eisenhower.

The President agrees to the international teams competing for the Eisenhower Trophy. The trophy is inscribed with the Council's governing principle "To foster friendship and sportsmanship among the Peoples of the World". Bobby Jones will captain team USA.

The teams will comprise of four players from each country with the lowest three out of the four scores counting on each of the four days of competition. In the event of a tie a playoff will commence the following day in the same format over 18-holes.

This was a very exciting development in the evolution of the game of golf. In New Zealand the only regular international competition had been against Australia and a new Commonwealth tournament had recently been established comprising teams of six from Great Britain & Ireland, Australia, Canada, South Africa and New Zealand. The first event was played in 1954 at St Andrews however these competitions were all match play events. The Eisenhower event would be a stroke play event on a truly international scale.

New Zealand at this stage in its golf evolution was going through a transition period where there were many new young talented players emerging on the scene and conversely most of the 1954 team members were coming to the end of their competitive playing days. The one exception was Stuart Jones. He had won the 1955 NZ Amateur championship. He was now in his late 20s and was firmly established as one of New Zealand's finest amateurs.

What should be the make-up of the New Zealand team to contest the inaugural Eisenhower tournament is best summed up in an in depth article written by *the Nineteenth*.

…I cannot help feeling that the time has come to cut the painter and to go bald headed for the group of youngsters who were so prominent at the NZ Amateur. There is a risk in this. One can never be quite sure that youngsters will live up to their promise and the golden glow that surrounds the bony young player of 19 too often turns out to be a worthless sheen. Moreover, it is foolish to give the young everything simply because they are young; and when you are confronted with the probability that a team made up of Silk, Woon, Jones and say W. W. Smith would almost certainly beat any ordinary team of youngsters it is difficult to be sure that a policy of deliberately encouraging the young is the right one.

The vital word at the moment is "ordinary." R. J. Charles has well and truly proved that he is anything but ordinary. In winning the amateur, E. J. McDougall also did something a little better than the usual and personally I shall always associate him and this tournament with the shot he played from a fairway bunker at the 18th to ensure that he and R. R. Newdick would win the amateur foursomes. There was courage and quality in every line of this stroke that even Nagle and Thomson, let alone the most experienced amateurs, could have done any better.

Though he has puzzling variations of form outside of Wellington, J. D. Durry also has proved himself, to my mind, unusually good and his effort in the Caltex Thousand went a long way to proving this. Durry's naiveté may preclude his development beyond a certain standard and it may be that he has already reached this; but his record as a youth is too good to justify his exclusion from any selection directly aimed at youth.

My last man for a four-man team would be Ian Harvey, of Waitikiri, Christchurch. He reached the last four of the amateur and he was the only amateur to score each of the four rounds of the Open in less than 80. There is more to him than this lone achievement He has been a good player since the age of 15 and at 20 is unusually rich in experience.

The Nineteenth would almost be proved correct. The NZ team selected to contest the Eisenhower in October was Charles, McDougall, Durry and Jones ahead of Harvey.

Just prior to the New Zealand team leaving for Scotland McDougall won his third consecutive Stewart Gold Cup.

E. J. McDougall of Pukekohe, although worried in almost equal proportions by his volatile temperament and the close proximity of the local player, G. R. Adams score, eventually conquered both to head the field at the Grange Golf Club over the weekend. This was his third win in succession, a fine effort considering the select company which contests the cup each season.

Results: Stewart Gold Cup - September 1958 - Grange Golf Club

1	**E. J. McDougall (Pukekohe)**	**74**	**72**	**75**	**72**	**293**
2	G. R. Adams (Grange)	73	75	72	76	296
3	W. J. Godfrey (Titirangi)	74	78	73	74	299
4	N. V. Edwards (Titirangi)	78	75	69	79	301
5	R. Pulman (Grange)	76	75	73	78	302
6=	R. R. Newdick (North Shore)	74	78	77	74	303
6=	J. P. Boon (Grange)	79	75	75	74	303

8   A. R. Ohlson (Waiuku)   75   74   77   79   305

The New Zealand team arrived well in advance of the Eisenhower commencing and played at many venues across England and Scotland including playing against a local team from Pitlochry where McDougall had learnt to play golf.

They arrived at St Andrews ready to go and felt confident of performing well after the completion of two practice rounds. The weather this particular October in Scotland was un-seasonally cold and wet and with the course measuring just shy of 7000 yards would prove to be a very difficult challenge indeed.

The Special correspondent to the New York Times, **FRED TUPPER**, wrote a comprehensive summary of the tournament to date after the completion of the third round under the headline;

New Zealand Team Captures Lead,

BRITISH, AUSSIES, IN THE TIE FOR THIRD

New Zealand Golfers Total 687-U.S. Gains Second by Stroke With 690

ST. ANDREWS, Scotland, Oct.10

The first world amateur golf team championship is wide open tonight.

Four nations are still in the running after fifty-four holes of the 72-hole event. The leaders' scores are New Zealand, 687; and the United States 690; Australia, 691, and the combined Britain-Northern Ireland team, 691.

The final eighteen holes will be played on the rugged Old Course tomorrow.

Australia catapulted into a threatening position today. Seventeen strokes behind the British-Irish leaders on opening day and nine behind at the half way mark, the young Aussie trio of Peter Toogood with seventy-one, Bruce Devlin seventy four, and Bob Stevens seventy-six, shot 221 today, the finest team daily aggregate so far, to tie the British-Irish for third place.

In front for the first time tonight was New Zealand. The hero youngsters who got 226 yesterday were even better today, posting 225. Twenty-one-year-old Eddie MacDougall, A 230-pound transplanted Scot, was in with a 72, and 22-year-old Bob Charles, though faltering at the finish, had a 76. A third New Zealander, 22-year-old Durry, scored a 77.

The 71 by Australia's Peter Toogood was the best round since the tournament began Wednesday.

Hyndman Cards an Eagle

The United States, six strokes behind in second place after the first round and four behind in third place last night, was still gaining. The Americans registered 225 today and trail by only three shots.

William Hyndman had a 73 and Charles Coe, Frank Taylor and Billy Joe Patton tallied 76 each.

Hyndman, a long hitter from Philadelphia, finally realized his potentialities. Big Bill, who hadn't a birdie on the first two days, got an eagle on the third at lunchtime.

A screaming drive down the middle on the 400-yard "cart-gate" left him a wedge to the green. He took aim and fired. The ball sat down, turned over once and dropped in for a deuce.

Another wedge at the twelfth left him a four-footer for a three. He rammed it in.

He was even par going to the seventeenth the dreaded "road hole." Deciding to play safe, he pulled out a No. 7 iron, switched to a six and regretted it.

The ball ran through the green and he got a six on his card. A ten-footer on the eighteenth gave Hyndman another Birdie. It was brilliant golf.

Dr. Frank Taylor, a California dentist, has been an enigma to the critical Scottish spectators. He is so pure in style and so intelligent in his shot execution that low scores seem inevitable. His first long putt of the tourney, a fifteen footer that dropped dead on the eighteenth for a birdie, meant a 76.

Patton Rallies with Pars

After a shuddering start, in which he collected five 5's in six holes, Billy Joe Patton of Morganton, N. C., got pars the rest of the way.

He lipped the cup with his putt for a possible deuce on the eleventh and lost it, then scrambled out of trouble with a tremendous pitch shot and five-yard putt to save par on the long fourteenth. His 76 was well earned.

Oklahoma's thin man, Charley Coe, solid all week, started poorly and finished well for his 76. He is third low man for the tourney so far with 227.

The darling of the Scottish gallery, a former commando, Reid Jack, is still in front. He posted 74 for a 223 total to keep the fading British and Irish delegation in contention.

Jaunty in plaid cap and short knickers, Jack played the old course as decreed by the book, running his pitches up to the pin and studiously angling his putts into the cup.

It was hard work though, and his score includes six one-putt greens. He never missed under eight feet all the way round.

Guy Wolstenholme had a 78, and Arthur Peronne a 79, but Ireland's Joe Carr, off to a frightful 41 at the turn, blazed down the home trail in 37 and the British-Irish had 230 from its best three scores of the day.

Canada, with 228, and South Africa, with 229, outplayed the mother country today.

MacDougall at Turn in 34

The first and last rounds of the short Scottish day were the best. MacDougall out early, reached the turn in 34, despite sporadic showers that slowed the ball's roll.

A cut drive sent him deep into the heather on the thirteenth and only a slick No. 7 iron that soared over the pine scrub and caught the corner of the green and saved him.

His 72 brought congratulations from Bobby Jones, the non-playing captain of the American team who was touring the course in an electric cart.

"Not too many of those," warned Bobby, "or you'll put us out."

Late in the day Toogood played a classic round for the Old Course. He made one mistake. A running shot up the bank of the eleventh green fell back. Next time it stuck.

He had a thirty-footer for a birdie 4 on the fifth, a ten-footer for a birdie three on the seventh, and a fifteen-footer for a birdie on the twelfth.

Two other putts missed by hair lines. "It should have been a 69", said Coe who was

17

Toogood's partner. "On any other course, who knows?"

Charles' Score Deceiving

Finally, Charles, the tourney's surprise, rounded the last bend. The Kiwi had rounds of 74 on Wednesday and Thursday for the low amateur score. He had 36 to the turn today.

Despite his scoring, Charles is not an impressive striker of the ball. The swing lapsed. He had a 7 at the fourteenth and was lucky to get it with a five yard putt.

He had 5's at the fifteenth and sixteenth. His 76 gave him 224 for three rounds, a shot behind Reid Jack.

3RD Round Results: Eisenhower Trophy - October 1958, St Andrews, Scotland

1. New Zealand				
R. J Charles	74	74	76	224
J. D Durry	81	78	77	236
S. G. Jones	81	75	80	236
E. J. McDougall	88	77	72	237
Total	**236**	**226**	**225**	**687**
2. United States of America				
William Hyndman III	79	77	73	229
Charles Coe	74	77	76	227
Billy Joe Patton	80	78	76	234
Dr Frank M Taylor, Jr	81	79	76	236
Total	**233**	**232**	**225**	**690**
3. Great Britain and Ireland				
R Reld Jack	72	77	74	223
Guy Wolstenhome	76	79	78	233
Arthur Perowne	81	78	79	238

Joseph Carr	79	84	78	241
Total	**227**	**234**	**230**	**691**

4. Australia

Doug Bachi	81	77	78	236
R. F. Stevens	82	77	76	235
B. W. Devlin	81	73	74	228
P. A. Toogood	84	76	71	231
Total	**244**	**226**	**221**	**691**

The Times correspondent would report that he had great reservations as to whether this young team could hold up against the might of the United States, Australia and Great Britain &Ireland. He would ultimately be proved correct in dramatic circumstances.

New Zealand were looking very comfortable and well in control heading into the back nine of the final round. Jones was first out for NZ in the morning and had scored 78 which should have laid a solid foundation for success.

McDougall was playing in the final group with Guy Wolstenholme and William Hyndman III. He was playing well and would finish with a 75. That left either Charles or Durry to score no worse than a 77 and New Zealand would be crowned world champions.

Charles, who was in contention for individual honors, however was having an un-characteristically bad day with the putter and finished with 81.

Durry on the other hand was well in control of his game when he stood on the 14th tee at two over 4s. Unfortunately for Durry, and New Zealand, he hit his tee shot on this famous par 5 hole out of bounds.

He then found the beardie bunkers with his second ball and eventually holed-out for a 10 and his struggles continued on the closing holes before he ultimately signed off for an 83.

Australia won after an 18-hole playoff against the United States on the

Monday. The Australian win remains the greatest come from behind victory in the history of the Eisenhower.

Great Britain & Ireland were third and New Zealand fourth just three strokes behind the winners.

The New Zealand team manager Mr. Jim Scoular would comment in his report to the New Zealand Council - *that there was great excitement on the final green as the outcome had come down to the final few holes with no clear front runner. The New Zealand team had proved very popular with the British media and public. Charles was singled out for his extraordinary good putting and no one was longer than McDougall off the tee.*

Results: 1958 Eisenhower, St Andrews, Scotland

1. Australia

Bruce Devlin	81	73	74	73	301
Peter Toogood	84	76	71	79	310
Robert Stevens	82	77	76	75	310
Douglas Bachli	81	77	78	79	315
Total	**244**	**226**	**221**	**227**	**918**

2. United States of America

William Hyndman III	79	77	73	72	301
Charles Coe	74	77	76	78	305
Billy Joe Patton	80	78	76	79	313
Dr Frank M Taylor, Jr	81	79	76	78	314
Total	**233**	**232**	**225**	**228**	**918**

3. Great Britain and Ireland

R Reld Jack	72	77	74	78	301
Guy Wolstenhome	76	79	78	77	310
Arthur Perowne	81	78	79	75	313
Joseph Carr	79	84	78	76	317
Total	**227**	**234**	**230**	**228**	**919**

4. New Zealand

Robert (Bob) Charles	74	74	76	81	305
Edward (Ted) McDougall	88	77	72	75	312
Stuart Jones	81	75	80	78	314
John Durry	81	78	77	83	319
Total	**236**	**226**	**225**	**234**	**921**

2 TIME TO TURN PROFESSIONAL

Soon after leaving school Ted had starting courting Leonie Pikett. They meet through golf. Leonie's father Howard was an active member of the Helensville Golf Club and was at various times club captain and president of the club. The club played host to a very popular annual stroke play event. It was at one of these events that Ted and Leonie meet. They married in December 1958 soon after the completion of the Eisenhower tournament.

Leonie had already been in the unenviable situation of having to take control of the household for her father and two older brothers on the family farm when her mother died when she was only fifteen years of age.

When her father re-married Leonie then trained as nurse and sadly had to nurse Ted's mother Jane who had taken seriously ill with cancer just before Ted was due to travel to Scotland. Ted had considered withdrawing from the Eisenhower however his mother insisted he travel. Jane died in January 1959.

Edward right from a young age had always harbored ambitions of turning professional. New Zealand by this time had developed quite an extensive professional circuit and, with Peter Thomson and Kel Nagle already regular visitors to New Zealand shores, a very competitive one at that. The-circuit however was not lucrative enough to earn a proper income but was none the less still an attractive proposition.

Ted had considered the idea of becoming an assistant professional at a club.

Instead he opted to take a position in sales with the Whangarei branch of the sporting goods company Wisemans. The owner of the company had immediately contacted McDougall on his return from Scotland and offered him seventeen pounds a week to be one the experts on golf for his company. McDougall jumped at the opportunity as it provided a secure income and he was permitted time off to compete on the New Zealand professional golf circuit.

Wisemans had been in New Zealand for over a decade and they were a very reputable company and boasted a team of up to six golf professionals and two teaching tennis professionals with indoor facilities to match.

Alex Murray who was born in Pitlochry, Scotland in 1910 and who was Jonny Murray's nephew arrived in New Zealand aged seventeen was also employed by Wisemans. He would become one of New Zealand's great professional golfers winning the NZ Open in 1935, 1939, 1947 and 1948.

It was to be a very successful and fruitful year. Ted competed in fourteen professional events finishing with five wins and including 12 top 10 finishes. He finished 14th in each of the two biggest events on the golfing calendar being the New Zealand Open and the Caltex sponsored event both played at the Paraparaumu links course. He earned total prize money of £623 for the year.

Ted's first tournament win as a professional came in the middle of the year at the Drysdale Ales sponsored tournament played on the Maungakiekie course in June. He shot rounds of 70 and 69.

The following week he won the Tauranga Invitational which he had also won as an amateur in 1957.

E. J. McDougall had his second win in professional golf when he took the Tauranga invitation title yesterday and the largest share of £200.

McDougall played an outstanding first round of 67, which included five birdies. This was the second best score at the links. A. Murray scored a sensational 64 in 1954.

Results: 7TH Tauranga Invitation Tournament (£200) - August 1959

1	**E. J. McDougall (Whangarei)**	**67**	**72**	**71**	**210**
2	A. C. Relph* (Rotorua)	73	72	73	218
3	A. E. Guy (Auckland)	71	75	73	219
4	F. X. Buckler (Hamilton)	75	72	73	220
5=	S. E. Cox (Auckland)	77	76	68	221
5=	R. A. Jackson (Auckland)	75	74	72	221
7	E. A. Southerden (Napier)	74	74	74	222
8	J. Cowley (Auckland)	73	75	77	225
9=	J. A. Parkinson (Tauranga)	75	73	78	226
9=	R. A. Court* (New Plymouth)	79	72	75	226

McDougall would then make it three in a row. The associated press would report;

Driving with tremendous power and putting consistently, the Whangarei professional E. McDougall won the sponsored golf tournament conducted by the New Plymouth Golf Club at its Ngamotu links over the weekend by a margin of one stroke from the Napier professional E. A. Southerden.

The total prize money was £200, the winner receiving £75. McDougall was steady through-out the tournament. He started off with 73 for the first round and then returned an excellent 70 for his second. This was the second best recorded eclipsed only by Southerden's first round. When the going become difficult yesterday McDougall appeared to be less hampered than many and returned a final round of 76 to give him a total of 219.

Southerden's first round revealed some outstanding golf. He was out in 32 and back in 34 to give him 66, easily the best round of the tournament. He could not hold his brilliant form, however, and his final two rounds took 77 to give him 220'.

Results: New Plymouth Golf Club Sponsored Tournament (£200) - September 1959

1	**E. J. McDougall (Whangarei)**	73	70	76	219
2	E. A. Southerden (Napier)	66	77	77	220
3	T. J. Jeffery*	73	71	78	222
4	F. X. Buckler (Hamilton)	72	76	76	224
5	J Kelly (Auckland)	76	72	77	225
6	R. R. Newdick* (Auckland)	71	74	82	227
7=	R. A. Jackson (Auckland)	72	80	76	228
7=	D. V. Southerland*	75	75	78	228
9=	M Busk (Palmerston North)	74	80	75	229
9=	B. M. Silk* (Wanganui)	72	79	78	229

In October, six weeks out from the NZ Open, McDougall played in the Auckland Open. The NZ Herald golf correspondent reported;

E. J. McDougall, the young professional, played one of the great rounds of recent times in New Zealand golf when he scored a 66 to win a decisive victory in the Auckland Open championship at the Auckland club's course at Middlemore yesterday.

The round to all intents and purposes equaled the course record which was set by Peter Thomson in the New Zealand Open in 1955. More materially, it catapulted McDougall from second place at the end of the third round at lunch-time to first place by no fewer than seven strokes at the end of play.

McDougall won the Dunlop Cup and £50.

Fierce and blustering winds tightened the kinks in the technique of a good many competitors during the first two rounds on Saturday and the faces which gazed at the scoreboard on Saturday evening were nearly as long as some of the scores.

By contrast, the conditions yesterday were as close to perfection as they are ever likely to be and they encouraged McDougall to give the finest display of sustained hitting of his short but by no means undistinguished career.

The round, so it seemed, was bound to come. After all sorts of scratching for the first nine holes of the first round, McDougall suddenly began to middle the ball. He all but scored an eagle two at the short tenth, his No. 4 wood carried the 11th green -270 yards from the tee- to a bunker but he still got a birdie 3 and at the 12ᵗʰ he scored another 3 with no trouble whatsoever.

No fewer than five times in a row did he score 3s, at the 17ᵗʰ he got another one-an eagle this time- and at the 18ᵗʰ his firm putt hit the back of the hole for yet another 3 but in some mysterious way managed to stop out of the hole.

So after taking 43 for the first nine, he was back in 33. He had another 33 for the homeward run in the third round yesterday morning. Then in the afternoon he set to work. This was his score:

Out: 4 4 4 4 4 4 3 3 4-34

In: 3 3 4 3 3 4 4 4 4-32

The only possible blemish was at the 12ᵗʰ hole where he could not manage to hole out with his first putt after putting his approach shot within five feet of the hole. Of no other shot would it be possible to offer any criticism. The drives were long, the seconds were ruled onto the pin and the putts sank sweetly out of sight with a minimum of fuss.

Best of all, McDougall had his volatile temperament completely under control. In all respects, this was the finest display of his career'.

Results: Auckland Open - October 1959

1	E. J. McDougall (Whangarei)	76	75	74	66	291
2	J. Kelly (Remuera)	75	75	77	71	298
3	A. E. Guy (unattached)	77	72	75	77	301
4	W. J. Godfrey* (Titirangi)	77	76	73	76	302
5=	R. A. Jackson (Akarana)	80	78	73	75	306
5=	R. W. Wilkinson (Howick).	73	78	75	80	306

7=	M. J. Brusk (Manawatu)	77	77	80	75	309
7=	F. X. Buckler (Lochiel)	77	80	75	77	309
7=	N. V. Edwards* (Titirangi)	78	75	78	78	309
10	G. M. Lees* (Titirangi)	81	74	77	78	310

Peter Thomson won the £1,000 Caltex sponsored event and also the NZ Open beating Kel Nagle in a playoff. Nagle had holed a 20 yard pitch shot for an eagle on the last to force a playoff.

Ted then won the final event of the year on the New Zealand professional circuit -the Lewis Motors sponsored 27-hole pro-am-held in December and conducted at the Pupuke golf course on Auckland's North Shore.

It had been more than a satisfactory rookie season for Edward. His total earnings for the year were more than double the national average salary and he was now in the enviable position of being able to build a brand new Fletcher home for his young family in Whangarei.

His golf game was progressing nicely and at the age of 22 he would have been confidently looking forward to an even better 1960 season.

Unbeknown to him however Wisemans under new management were experiencing financial difficulties and were about to file for bankruptcy and close down. Ted was now unemployed.

Edward was born in Dundee, Scotland in 1937. His parents were Edward Frank McDougall and Jane Hendry. Ted's father was an only child and came from Moulin near Pitlochry. Ted's mother Jane had five brothers and three sisters.

The Hendry's lived in a commuter town to Dundee, Monifieth. Jane's two oldest brothers were golf professionals and club makers. John "Jock" Hendry was born in 1895 and did his club making apprenticeship with Alec Simpson and then worked for J.C. Smith until 1923.

William the oldest boy was appointed club maker and professional at the Malone Golf Club in Belfast however after the start of a promising career he died of pneumonia in 1921.

It was during this period that there were a number of pioneering emigrants from Monifieth to America. The export list from Monifieth started with Willie Still followed by The Levies, Willie Lorimer, Willie and Colin Kidd and Edward's uncle "Jock" Hendry. They were all to become famous names in American golf circles.

Jock Hendry's decision to immigrate to Minnesota was influenced by Tom Vardon who had immigrated to America in 1911. This had been soon after Tom had caddied for his older brother Harry to victory at the 1911 Open Championship held at Royal St Georges, England. Tom was the professional there at the time. It was on the eve of his final round that Tom informed Harry that he had accepted a position as the professional at the Onwestia Country Club just north of Chicago.

Harry and Tom were very close and while Harry was disappointed by his brother's decision he none the less fully supported him. It was time for Tom to break free from living in his older brother's shadow and make his own way in life in America.

In 1916 Tom Vardon was appointed the professional at the infamous White Bear Yacht Club just north of St. Paul, Minnesota. The White Bear Yacht Club is where in 1921 F. Scott Fitzgerald and his wife, Zelda, rented a room for the summer where he could relax in quiet surroundings and write. However their holiday was cut short after they were requested to leave after indulging in far too much drinking and fighting.

The setting and his experiences of the White Bear Yacht Club would be the inspiration for Fitzgerald's short story "Winter Dreams" and his book, "The Great Gatsby". It would also be the source of his acclaimed quote, "The rich are different to you and I."

Jock Hendry's first role when he arrived in St Paul in 1923 was as the professional at the Midland Hills Country Club where he remained for two years until, on the recommendation of Tom Vardon, he was appointed the professional at the Town and Country Club in St Paul. Ted McDougall's uncle Jock would remain here until his retirement in 1960.

Jock was a very good golf player in his own right. He competed in the 1924 US Open and the 1930 US Open held at Interlachen, Minnesota. In the qualifying rounds Jock was first off with Tom Vardon and they both qualified with Jock eventually finishing tied 58th. This was the venue and year for Bobby Jones's third victory on the way to winning the grand slam of golf.

Jock won the Minnesota State Open in 1929 and was inducted into the Minnesota Golf Hall of Fame in 1984. Jock also played in an exhibition match with the great George Von Elm at Town & Country where von Elm would shoot a par breaking 70.

In 1952 PGA members and sports writers voted von Elm the 10th most important amateur golfer in US history. He beat Bobby Jones in the final of the 1926 US Amateur Championships but he is perhaps best known for his second place finish in the 1931 US Open.

He birdied the last hole in regulation play to force a play-off against Billy Burke. He would eventually lose the play-off by 1 shot after two sets of 36 holes were required to eventually find a winner. It remains the longest play-off in US Open history. In winning this event Billy Burke became first professional to win using steel shafts.

George Von Elm's career would not be without controversy. In 1922 the United States Golf Association banned him for one year for allegedly receiving expense money from his old club friends in Salt Lake City. He would eventually give up his amateur status in 1930 to become a "Business Man Golfer" believing golf should be a gentlemanly pursuit, not a professional career.

Jock was still the professional at the Town and Country Club in 1960 at the same time his nephew Edward was unemployed in New Zealand.

Two of Jock's sisters, Ted's mother Jane and Margaret, lived in New Zealand. He also had a brother Gordon in New Zealand. In January of 1959 Jock's younger sister Jane passed away at the early age of 59. In July 1959 Margaret also passed away. They both lived in the Pukekohe region in New Zealand.

Jock had returned to Scotland in 1952 to visit family and see Jane's family leave for New Zealand on the *Captain Cooke's* maiden voyage. He gave Ted a new golf bag, putter and four wood. He also took him to a game of rugby at Murrayfield.

These actions would indicate he was informed of his wider family happenings. It does appear however that Jock did not know about his nephew's exploits at St Andrews in 1958 and that Edward had subsequently turned professional and was making encouraging progress as a professional.

Conversely it appears Edward did not know what his uncle Jock had achieved in Minnesota and the connections that he potentially could have developed in America.

There does appear to be a big missed opportunity here. It would not be unreasonable to assert McDougall's game was only improving the more he played. He had already, at a very young age, achieved considerable success.

Jock was his uncle and greatly respected in the United States. He had mentored a number of young professionals in Minnesota.

Had they each fully understood each-others circumstances then it would not be unreasonable to assume McDougall could have taken his family to Minnesota where he would have been welcomed by his uncle and where his game would have been ideally suited to the playing conditions he would likely encounter in America.

Instead, unable to find suitable employment in New Zealand that would allow Ted to play professional golf, he made the decision to seek reinstatement as an amateur.

Ted had indeed approached two clubs in Auckland to be an assistant professional however at the time there existed considerable resentment towards "unattached" professionals and he was subsequently turned down.

In 1960 Ted moved his family from Whangarei to Takapuna on Auckland's North Shore and found a job as a clerk in an oil company. During his compulsory two year stand down period from competition he played very little golf.

Meanwhile whilst McDougall was out of the amateur game Bob Charles would have another fine performance at the Eisenhower conducted on the Merion course in the United States. New Zealand finished 5th and Jack

Nicklaus would lead the United States to a comprehensive victory with his amazing individual performance.

Bob Charles turned professional in 1961. The New Zealand team for Japan in 1962 included Stuart Jones who had won the 1961 NZ Amateur, Ross Newdick who had won the 1960 NZ Amateur, and Walter Godfrey who at the age of 16 is the youngest ever winner of the NZ Amateur when he won in 1958 whilst the NZ team was in Scotland.

They would be joined by Ross Murray. New Zealand finished fourth with Godfrey and Newdick being the stand out performers for New Zealand both finishing tied 11th on the individual standings.

Gary Cowan from Canada was the leading individual on a score of 280.

Results: 1960 Eisenhower, Merion, USA

1. United States of America

Jack Nicklaus	66	67	68	68	269
Deane Beman	71	67	69	75	282
William Hyndman III	71	76	67	75	289
Robert Gardner	71	71	68	79	289
Total	**208**	**205**	**203**	**218**	**834**

2. Australia

Bruce Devlin	74	70	70	74	288
Eric Routley	72	75	72	72	291
Edward (Ted) Ball	77	75	73	76	301
Jack Coogan	73	80	74	78	305
Total	**219**	**220**	**215**	**222**	**876**

3. Great Britain and Ireland

Michael Bonallack	73	72	73	78	296
Guy Wolstenhome	71	75	76	75	297
Douglas Sewell	74	73	76	74	297
Joseph Carr	78	70	72	81	301
Total	**218**	**215**	**221**	**227**	**881**

5. New Zealand

Robert (Bob) Charles	70	75	70	76	291
Walter Godfrey	74	76	74	77	301
Stuart Jones	80	74	76	80	310
Ross Newdick	73	76	82	82	313
Total	**217**	**225**	**220**	**233**	**895**

Results: 1962 Eisenhower, Japan

1. United States of America

Richard Sikes	69	76	69	69	283
Deane Beman	70	80	70	66	286
Labron Harris, Jr	73	77	72	70	292
Billy Joe Patton	74	73	72	81	300
Total	**212**	**226**	**211**	**205**	**854**

2. Canada

Gary Cowan	68	71	72	69	280
Nick Weslock	71	73	75	73	292
William Wakemen	76	73	72	78	299
Robert Wylie	77	78	80	69	304
Total	**215**	**217**	**219**	**211**	**862**

3. Great Britain and Ireland

Ronald Shade	75	66	74	76	291
Michael Bonallack	74	80	69	70	293
A.C. Sandler	79	76	72	70	297
Martin Christmas	73	80	73	78	304
Total	**222**	**222**	**214**	**216**	**874**

4. New Zealand

Walter Godfrey	69	80	73	73	295
Ross Newdick	74	76	72	73	295
Ross Murray	75	72	76	76	299
Stuart Jones	77	76	73	81	307
Total	**218**	**224**	**218**	**222**	**882**

7. Australia

Phillip Billings	81	72	75	67	295
Tom Crow	77	77	72	73	299
Kevin Donohoe	74	77	73	78	302
Douglas Bachli	79	76	78	79	312
Total	**230**	**225**	**220**	**218**	**893**

3 ROME 1964

One of the first tournaments McDougall played in after being re-instated as an amateur was the 1962 Auckland provincial match play championship. He won this in convincing style by beating Walter Godfrey 1up in the semi-final and Ross Newdick 6 and 4 in the final. Ted followed this up by winning the Auckland Champion of Champions.

He was now a certainty for selection for the Auckland team to play in the Freyberg Rose Bowl interprovincial tournament in Dunedin. He would however have to play at No. 3 in the team of six behind Ross Newdick and Walter Godfrey who were now current New Zealand representatives.

The team performed well at the Otago Golf Club in Dunedin however Canterbury would prevail over Auckland to decide the ultimate winner of the Freyberg Rose Bowl. One of the talking points of the tournament was the match between K. D. Foxton and E. J. McDougall.

Foxton won this match however on 7th hole, known as the 'Glen', which was their 15th hole for this match, McDougall drove his tee shot to the astonishment of the onlookers through the back of the 388yd par 4 hole and into the back bunker. His golf ball had travelled almost 400 yds.

Even McDougall, who it is customary for him to hit his golf ball extraordinary distances, was moved to comment "Boy, what a drive".

One of McDougall's strengths obviously was his power. In later years he would learn to temper this power which could be troublesome. His strategy in his early years was essentially to hit his tee shot as far as he could, find the ball, and go from there.

Sandy Wilson, a member of the Pitlochry Golf Club, recalls watching the match in 1958 between Pitlochry and New Zealand where he witnessed McDougall hit his opening tee shot into the cross bunkers some 310 yards away….uphill!!.

Although McDougall was playing some good golf his play was still erratic and he had not yet attained the same level of performance he had attained from 1957 through 1959. Getting back in the New Zealand team was not going to be an easy task.

Ross Newdick and Walter Godfrey were now the stars of New Zealand Golf and then you had Ross Murray emerging on the scene and Stuart Jones still playing as well as ever at home. John Durry, who had recently returned home after some overseas experience, was also playing good golf. Bob Charles by now had turned professional after another successful performance at the 1960 Eisenhower at Merion.

The other thing Ted had to contend with was a certain amount of resentment in the media that as he had previously been a professional golfer he should not therefore be eligible to play for New Zealand despite the fact he had been stood down for two years.

He would therefore have to perform at an even higher level than what would normally be expected to make the New Zealand team and even then he would continue to receive unfair criticism for several years to come before he would eventually win over the media and the NZ public.

The New Zealand team had performed well in 1960 at Merion finishing fifth with Charles having another top five individual performance.

The stand out performance was of course that of Jack Nicklaus who rated his performance in 1960 at Merion as possibly the best performance of his entire illustrious career when he shot 269 for four rounds. The next best individual was Dean Beman on 282.

Ross Newdick would however comment on his return to New Zealand that McDougall was longer off the tee than Nicklaus.

The selectors picked a fairly predictable team for the 1962 Eisenhower to be played in Japan. There was only one change from the team that played in Merion with Murray coming in for Charles and the other three being Godfrey, Newdick and Jones.

New Zealand had another good performance in Japan finishing fourth again frustratingly just outside of the medal table. Both Godfrey and Newdick played to a very high standard. Had Godfrey not had a second round 80 he surely would have finished in the top five for individual honors. Murray was a solid performer in his first Eisenhower tournament however Jones would again perform well below the standard of golf he produced at home.

The 1963 season did not begin well for Ted. Ross Newdick had convinced Ted to move from the Helensville Golf Club to Muriwai, where he played, and although Ted won the Muriwai club championship, by beating Jack Oliver in the final, he had to sit most of the middle part of the year out as he underwent treatment for his aching back.

He was therefore not even a possibility to make the New Zealand team to play in the third Commonwealth tournament in Sydney Australia. He was also unavailable to play for Auckland in the interprovincial tournament due to injury.

The second half of the year would be kinder to McDougall. He finished third in the Stewart Gold Cup behind Newdick and Malloy and played in an Auckland team against Great Britain and Ireland and Canada. These teams had a made a detour on their way to Australia and used this match as a warm up event.

The New Zealand journalist T. P. McLean wrote a very entertaining article on the encounter under the headline COMMONWEALTH GOLF STARS IN AUCKLAND;

To all intents and purposes, it was Commonwealth Day at the Auckland Golf Club yesterday and to deepen the significance of a meeting of British, Canadian and Auckland amateur golfers, one of the Canadians, D. Silverberg, scored a hole-in-one with a ball he had just taken out of the wrapper.

In honor of the visitation by the British and Canadian teams, which next week will compete in the Commonwealth tournament, the third of its kind, at Royal Sydney, the Auckland Golf Association arranged various fixtures.

First, the British on Saturday played a friendly match at Muriwai course, and were so much impressed by the possibilities an eminent official, Mr. G. H. Micklem, chairman of the championship committee of the Royal and Ancient Club of St Andrews, afterwards prophesied that within 25 years six or eight courses would be in use on the dune country on which this course has been built.

Mr. Micklem's prediction would not eventuate. The course has recently been redesigned to take account of erosion from the Tasman Sea.

Yesterday things became a little more serious when the Auckland representative side played, and was defeated by, the British at Middlemore. Auckland won all three of the four-ball matches in the morning, but in the afternoon the British swept the singles rubbers by five to one.

Coincidentally, the Canadians, after spending 16 hours travelling about 6000 miles across the Pacific were committed to a purely friendly four-ball fixture against an Auckland side. This ended in the Canadians winning two rubbers and halving the other.

It was this match which was given peculiar distinction when Silverberg holed out his tee-shot at the 120-yard 10th hole.

He had plucked a new American-sized ball from his bag, so that it would sit down better into the wind, and was gratified in the extreme when his shot with a wedge carried the ball on to the green and thence, with a couple of skips and hops, into the hole.

But the other match was the thing, and in this only two Aucklanders, R. R. Newdick, the international, in the morning, and the young Samoan, F. T. Malloy, in the afternoon played with real distinction. Newdick's 72 (38-34) of the morning included two or three missed chances on putts, one of them quite a short one on the sixth, but it was fine golf under the hard and dry conditions.

Malloy in the afternoon defeated the English champion, M. Bonallack, with birdies at 5th, 14th and 17th holes, and with only one stroke slipped to par at the 15th. He was out in 35 and even fours for the second half and that under the conditions, was really fine going.

Almost certainly the most impressive player of the British players was R. D. B. M.

Shade, who, because of his portmanteau of given names and the quality of his play, is known in the golfing fraternity as "Right Down the Blinking Middle" Shade.

A tall, notably contained sort of player, he put paid to Newdick with a birdie at the 7th and three consecutive birdies at the 15th, 16th, and 17th holes at the tail of the match; and you would have to travel many a golf course to see a finer iron than the one he sent soaring on to the green at the 430-yard 15th.

The amusing card of the British team was S. C. Saddler, a 28-year-old baker, who stood precisely 5 feet 4 inches high, and who would weigh, wringing wet, maybe 9 ½ stone. A bouncy, jaunty little man from beyond the border-he and E. J. McDougall could remember competing in a boys' tournament at Pitlochry, or some such place - Saddler laid into the ball much as Macduff laid into Macbeth, and the distances were not only surprising, they were quite staggering.

By one little byplay, the British captain, C. D. Lawrie, discovered that New Zealand can also produce crisp folding money. Having played in the morning and driven the 270-yard 11th green, Micklem wagered 10 to 1 in 10s that Lawrie could not perform the feat when he played in the afternoon. Lawrie did, within seven feet of the hole, what was more, and Micklem paid up like a man. Two or three holes later Lawrie played a shank to end all shanks, and the ball shivered among the timbers; but the folding money was safe, for no one had thought to wager against him on this sort of shot.

It was getting late when Newdick drove a ball into a tree at the 16th, gallantly climbed the trunk and swiped the ball onward. But Shade, as before, was right down the blinking middle and that was the end of Newdick.

Scores:-

GREAT BRITAIN v AUCKLAND

R. D. B. M. Shade and A. Thirlwell lost to G. M. Lees and K. R. Hankin, 2 and 1; G. H. Michlem and P. Green lost to E. J. McDougall and B. Vezich, 2 and 1; M. Bonallack and S. C. Sandler lost to R. R. Newdick and F. T. Malloy, 6 and 4.

Green beat Hankin, 4 and 2; Lawrie beat Lees, 2 and 1; Thirlwell beat Vezich, 2 and 1; Saddler beat McDougall 4 and 2; Bonallack lost to Malloy, 3 and 2; Shade beat Newdick, 2 and 1.

CANADA v AUCKLAND

F. Alexander and D. Silverberg beat B. McNiven and B. K. Osmand, 1 up; B. Ticehurst and W. Wakeman halved with N. W. Osmand and B. A. Burton; N. Weslock and G. Cowan beat N. F. Dowden and I. D. W. Dyer, 5 and 4.

Later in 1963 Ted performed well in the NZ Open and Amateur at Belmont, Wanganui. This was the last year that the NZ Amateur and NZ Open were played as a combined event. He scored 289 and qualified high up on the amateur side and would eventually bow out in the quarter final to the local player H.R. Carver. This was a good sign however that McDougall was now on the way to performing at a level he had been accustomed to in the late 1950's.

He then began the 1964 season with a second place finish in the Tauranga Invitational.

Results: Tauranga Invitational Tournament January 1964 (£250)

1	T. Leech* (Taupo)	70	72	65	207
2	**E. J. McDougall* (Muriwai)**	**70**	**68**	**70**	**208**
3	W. J. Godfrey (Unattached)	69	67	72	208
4	B Croxon (Manawatu)	71	70	71	212
5	D. K. Boone* (Springfield)	72	74	69	215
6	K. H. Hankin* (Titirangi)	70	75	75	220
7=	D. Clark (Rotorua)	73	76	72	221
7=	P. A. Maude* (Otorohanga)	76	69	76	221
9=	N. F. Hayden (Manukau)	75	76	72	223
9=	T. A. Brady (Miramar)	73	73	77	223

McDougall continued his good form into 1964 and performed well enough in the Auckland trials to be selected No. 1 for the Auckland team to contest the Freyberg Rose Bowl to be played at Hokowhitu in Palmerston North. Godfrey and Newdick had by now both turned professional.

He had a satisfactory tournament as he was unbeaten after four rounds but this was tempered by losses to Durry and Murray in his last two matches. The Freyberg was won by the home team Manawatu-Wanganui.

The venue for the 1964 World Amateur Teams (Eisenhower) was Oligiata, Italy. There was a lot of media interest in the selection of the New Zealand team as it was a little more wide-open than in previous years.

With both Godfrey and Newdick having turned professional since the Japan Eisenhower there were effectively two new spots available as Jones and Murray were considered certainties.

Essentially selection for the NZ team was based on the following criteria;

1) Play well enough in your provincial trials to be selected either 1 or 2 in your provincial team and perform well at the Freyberg Rose Bowl tournament.

2) Perform well in the NZ Amateur or the NZ Open.

3) Perform well in either the South Island or North Island stroke play events. It was not compulsory to play in both but to be considered for selection you needed to have played in at least one of these events.

The NZ Amateur & Open was traditionally played in November being a month after the completion of the Eisenhower hence it was always the odd years that were more important to perform well in. McDougall had achieved a satisfactory result in the Amateur in 1963 and produced a satisfactory performance in the Freyberg Rose Bowl however neither of these performance would warrant national selection at this stage. He needed a top performance at the North Island stroke play to have a realistic chance of selection.

Stuart Jones opted not to play in the North Island by virtue of his win at the South Island stroke play. He had also won the 1961 and 1962 NZ Amateurs hence he would have been considered a certainty for selection.

Durry also opted not to play as he had won the Amateur in 1963 therefore also odds on to make the team.

Ross Murray, who many would have also considered a certainty, chose not to play in the South Island stroke play and was subsequently summoned by the selectors to play in the North Island stroke play. He lived in the South Island. The North Island that year was to be played in Whangarei which was about as far north as you can get in New Zealand!

If Ross Murray had a top five finish the rest of the field were virtually playing for the last spot on the New Zealand team. The media believed the two leading contenders were 21 year old Terry Leech from Taupo and Ted McDougall and whilst both McDougall and Leech had some strong performances in various pro-am events over the summer it was Leech who the media believed had the inside running going into this tournament.

Another obstacle McDougall had to overcome were the rumors circulating that he would not be considered for selection because he had previously been a professional.

As it turned out McDougall with a final round 70, the best round of the tournament, and a four round total of 293 completed a three stroke victory over Ross Murray.

Leech who was only two shots behind McDougall going into the final round had a disappointing 79 for a total of 304 to finish eleven shots behind McDougall.

Results: North Island Stroke Play Championship - August 1964 (Mt Denby, Whangarei)

1	E. J. McDougall (Muriwai)	73	75	75	70	293
2	R. C. Murray (Russley)	75	73	74	74	296
3=	B. Vezich (Titirangi)	72	79	72	76	299
3=	J. G. Stern (Manukau)	76	73	73	77	299
5	F. Malloy (Akarana)	79	77	71	73	300
6	J. P. Means (Castlecliffe)	80	72	78	71	301
7	T. Leech (Taupo)	75	74	76	79	304

8	B. T. Boys (Hamilton)	76	79	75	75	305
9	D. J. Ryan (Hamilton)	78	76	79	74	307
10	D. K. Boone (Springfield)	79	82	74	73	308

McDougall therefore secured the last spot on the New Zealand team alongside Murray, Jones and Durry. There was an unusual amount of comment and criticism on McDougall's selection for this team. One person in particular, Mr. Jack Black a prominent golf personality from Wellington, was particularly scathing with McDougall's selection.

This criticism however was counter balanced by some more balanced journalism from Jim Wallace who would continue to promote the more positive aspects of McDougall's game and his proven ability to produce high class performances on the biggest of stages such as the World Amateur Teams Championship.

On the way to Rome, New Zealand played their customary pre Eisenhower match against Australia for the Sloan Morpeth Trophy. The Eisenhower trophy is typically played in October. As this is not long after the southern hemisphere winter it is imperative to get some top level competition under your belt and brush off the cob webs prior to competing in the Eisenhower.

This particular year New Zealand played Australia in Sydney. With little preparation New Zealand were soundly beaten five and a half to a half. McDougall got the half against Phillip Billings to avoid a complete white wash. Despite this disappointing result it had none the less served its purpose of some top level competition on a golf course considered to have many characteristics similar to what they would encounter at Olgiata.

There was a little scare when McDougall required treatment for a painful right elbow. *An injection was administered, and when 40 minutes later McDougall drove one of the longest balls from the first tee ever seen at Pennant Hills, and the complaint did not recur during the trip.*

New Zealand made a slow start at Olgiata despite McDougall scoring an adventurous even par 72 in the opening round. With the other two counting scores from Durry (76) and Murray (77) for a combined total of 225 New Zealand were in eleventh place and eleven strokes behind the leading team of Great Britain and Ireland.

In the second round New Zealand moved into third place after a brilliant 70 from Ross Murray. McDougall backed up with a 76 and Jones improved on his first round 80 with a 77. Durry had the non-counting score of 81.

In the third round New Zealand dropped one place to fourth. Murray and Durry shot 76 and McDougall was the third counting score on 77. Jones was non-counting with 78.

Starting the last round New Zealand were six strokes behind the leaders Great Britain & Ireland and only one shot behind Canada and the United States.

Wind and rain buffeted the field of 132, representing 33 countries, for the second successive day.

New Zealand played extremely well in the conditions with McDougall and Murray leading the way with impressive 74s and Durry contributing a solid 75 in the torrid conditions. New Zealand had moved ahead of the United States but come up just shy of Canada with Great Britain hanging on to win.

New Zealand had finished third. It was their best effort to date in the World Amateur Team Championship. Australia finished ten shots behind New Zealand.

Ross Murray finished third equal with a total score of 297 in the individual standings and Ted McDougall seventh equal with 299. None of the four players in the winning Great Britain &Ireland team broke 300.

Both McDougall and Murray had finished ahead of some of the great amateurs in world golf including Ronald Shade and Michael Bonallack of Britain, Dean Beman of America and Gary Cowan of Canada.

John Durry made valuable contributions with 76 in the third round and 75 in the last round. Jones was the only player to have a disappointing tournament. It would forever be a mystery why Stuart Jones could not take his domestic form to the same level at the Eisenhower competition. R.E.M. would report in the press *maybe he tried a fraction too hard and got over tense.*

One of the frustrations for the New Zealand team whilst they were away from home were the financial arrangements imposed by the Reserve Bank of New Zealand. Generally the New Zealand Golf Association covers all the players travelling costs however the Reserve Bank only allowed £7 per day per player.

Under the headline **"Australia Rescued Tourists"** the following was reported on their return home.

But for the Australian Golf Union coming to the rescue with funds, the New Zealand golf team would have been extremely financially embarrassed during their trip to and from Rome for the world amateur championship.

Team members who returned yesterday were asked to comment on the restrictions the Reserve Bank had placed on overseas expenditure.

"It cost at least £7 a day for our accommodation," said John Durry, "even before we started to think about meals."

Said R. C. Murray: "I couldn't even afford to buy any gifts to bring back for my family."

E. J. McDougall commented that soft drinks were 3s 4p a bottle and no matter what sort of lunch was eaten the cover charge was well over £1. Caddies cost as much as £2 a round.

All members agreed that these were minimum standards and Durry felt that the allowance should be at least £20 a day for normal living instead of the £7 that had been allowed.

Things got so bad that there were insufficient funds to meet the hotel bill in Sydney and the Australian authorities came to the rescue at the last minute.

"The Reserve Bank restrictions made us horribly short," said Durry, "and to be quite honest it was most embarrassing at times".

Results: 1964 Eisenhower, Rome

1. Great Britain and Ireland

Ronald D. B. M. Shade	70	81	74	75	300
Michael Lunt	72	76	79	74	301
Rodney Foster	72	79	75	75	301
Michael Bonallack	80	76	77	78	311
Total	**214**	**231**	**226**	**224**	**895**

2. Canada

Keith Alexander	76	75	72	74	297
Nick Weslock	74	72	75	77	298
Douglas Silverberg	74	80	78	73	305
Gary Cowan		85	79	74	
Total	**224**	**227**	**225**	**221**	**897**

3. New Zealand

Ross Murray	77	70	76	74	297
Ted McDougall	72	76	77	74	299
John Durry	76	81	76	75	308
Stuart Jones	80	77	78	79	314
Total	**225**	**223**	**229**	**223**	**900**

6. Australia

Phillip Billings	76	76	75	77	304
Tom Crow	72	78	76	77	303
Kevin Hartley		76	78	74	
B. Baker	75		79	79	
Total	**223**	**230**	**229**	**228**	**910**

4 MEXICO 1966

The NZ Amateur during this period was typically played in November being roughly a month after the completion of the Eisenhower. In 1964 it was also the first time that the amateur event was not combined with the New Zealand Open which was moved to a later date. The Amateur event this year was to be played at St. Andrews in Hamilton which is only two hours' drive south of Auckland just over the Bombay Hills.

Ted had returned home from Rome to be told that due to a down turn in business he had to be reluctantly let go by the drain laying firm he had been employed by.

It was not exactly the homecoming he was expecting. He had a wife and by now three children aged under five years of age to support. He was now unemployed and flat broke.

The great New Zealand journalist T. P. McLean reporting from St Andrews wrote in the NZ Herald explained it as such:

E. J. McDougall, the Aucklander who was an unexpected and successful selection in the New Zealand golf team which recently finished third in the Eisenhower Trophy in Rome, will not play in any further tournaments of the season. He has withdrawn from the New Zealand Open at Christchurch and has not entered the other sponsored tournaments of the professional circuit. McDougall said yesterday he was looking for a job. Some weeks ago he gave up his job as an insurance agent and for the period before the selection of the team for Rome was working at ditch-digging - an occupation which helped him to cut his poundage by about two stone from his mountainous weight of 18 stone 7lb. On his return from Rome, however, he discovered that his employment had ceased. As a married man with children and as a man who has only drawn one day's pay in the last five or six weeks because of golf, McDougall has per forcedly withdrawn from all competitive golf until at least in the new year.

Ted none the less had somehow found the means to at least play in the New Zealand Amateur. It was to be a fruitful week in more ways than one. Burt Sutcliffe a famous NZ cricketer was a keen golfer and a member of the St Andrews club offered to caddy for McDougall for the week.

McDougall played well and beat John Durry in the quarter final. He then prevailed over Brian Boys in the semi-final to set up an intriguing final against Stuart Jones.

Unfortunately for Ted, Sutcliffe couldn't caddy for him in the final due to a cricket engagement outside of town. Another equally amiable gentleman from New Plymouth would caddy instead.

All was going according to plan when he stood on the 34th tee (16th hole) 2up with three holes to play. Both hit good drives. Jones hit first from the fairway onto the front of green some 60 feet short of the back pin placement. McDougall rifled a seven iron straight at the flag however the ball finished in the fringe just behind the pin but still only 15 feet away. Jones putted first up to about 6 feet short.

McDougall has an immaculate short game and if he is not on the green will always chip rather than take the putter however on this occasion he allowed his caddy to talk him out of chipping. He took the putter instead and putted up to about 4 feet past the hole. Jones made his six footer and McDougall missed his return 4 footer.

McDougall then made a hash of the tricky 17th and they halved the last in par threes. They had finished all square for the 36-holes of regulation play. On the 37th-hole McDougall, unfortunately, pushed his drive out of bounds. The boundary is very tight down the right side because of its close proximity to the houses that line the first fairway. Jones had now won his 5th NZ Amateur title and McDougall was cruelly denied what would have been his second.

Good fortune however would come McDougall's way in the form of a gentleman by the name of Nelson Robinson. He was a very influential figure in Tokoroa in the South Waikato and he was on the lookout for high performing golfer who could bring success to the Waikato golf team in the national interprovincial tournament.

He arranged and offered Ted a job as a senior clerk at New Zealand's largest publicly listed company NZ Forest Products Ltd an international pulp and paper company. This was too good an opportunity to turn down and the family would soon be settled into a new chapter in their lives in Tokoroa.

This new career move would provide Ted's family with financial security and in addition give McDougall the opportunity and enough time off to enable him to play for his new adopted province and New Zealand.

John Davies, the New Zealand Olympic athletics representative, was already employed at NZFP. He encouraged Ted to get fit by taking up running as reported in the local paper under the headline; DETERMINED BID TO GET FIT - *E. J. McDougall is a golfer who really takes his sport seriously.*

Eighteen stone, six foot-plus McDougall, who is today playing for the Waikato golf team against Hawkes Bay, this week ran the six miles from Tokoroa to his place of work at Kinleith several times.

As well as the runs he has cut potatoes and bread out of his copious diet in a determined effort to "get fit."

Laughingly he described his decision to start running home from work as a method of "sharpening up" for golf. He said the idea was suggested to him by John Davies.

McDougall's form at the start of the 1965 season continued on from where 1964 had finished at the conclusion of the Amateur championship. He was now in a new town and province and it was important he started the season well, particularly in the Waikato trials, to enable selection at the top of the order for the interprovincial tournament to be played in May at Waitikiri in Canterbury territory.

He did that by winning his first of five Waikato Stroke Play titles. His score of seven under par 281 was very convincing indeed. Brian Boys finished next on 285 and S.M. Leech was the only other player to break 300 on 296. This result ensured McDougall was selected No. 1 for the six man team to contest the Freyberg Rose Bowl.

Results: Waikato Stroke Play - April 1965 (St Andrews, Hamilton)

1	E. J. McDougall	69	69	70	73	281
2	B. T. Boys	73	69	72	71	285
3	S. M. Leech	76	75	75	70	296
4	B. Stevens	72	71	79	78	300
5	P. M. Maude	76	80	73	72	301
6	G. C. Stevenson	77	75	77	75	304
7	J. T. Boys	70	78	78	80	306
8	K. Haggie	77	78	76	77	308
9	W. Fox	78	77	80	74	309
10	M. Thompson	79	80	76	76	311

The Freyberg Rose Bowl at this time was contested between the twelve provincial golf associations that existed at the time. The competition is a match play event played over six rounds. The seeded draw is determined by the results of the previous year's tournament. This is not an easy tournament to win and for the majority of the 72 players participating it is the highlight on their golfing calendar.

Waikato had previously never won the Freyberg Rose Bowl and it would almost be a honey moon start for McDougall and his new look Waikato team. After five rounds of the tournament both the Waikato and Canterbury teams had a perfect record of five straight wins. They would play each other in the deciding sixth and final round to determine the outcome of the Freyberg Rose Bowl.

As it transpired the ultimate outcome would be determined by the outcome of the match between Ross Murray and Ted McDougall at the top of the order. Going into this match McDougall had five straight convincing wins including beating both John Durry and Stuart Jones along the way.

Ross Murray was also almost as equally as impressive with 4 wins and a halved match against Frank Malloy from Auckland. McDougall however would find trouble during the middle part of their match and it would be Murray who would prevail 3 and 1 to secure a victory for Canterbury.

Although McDougall and Waikato had come up just short of their ultimate goal it had none the less been a very satisfactory campaign for McDougall and his new adopted province.

The next major event on the golfing calendar was the NZ Amateur to be played on the Miramar links course adjourning the Wellington airport. This is one of the most exposed and windiest parts of not only New Zealand but the world. Wellington is recognized as the fourth windiest city in the world.

Miramar along with the Paraparaumu links course, a 45 minute drive north of Wellington, would be regarded as New Zealand's only true links courses as only a Scotsman would truly appreciate.

Miramar has been revamped in recent times as the airport next door reclaimed more land from the golf course however Miramar has a proud history and is regarded as very good test of one's golfing skills in extreme windy conditions in true links fashion.

At this point in McDougall's career he had not had a lot of experience playing links golf. His golf game, which is based on a strong powerful fade off the tee, was not ideal in extreme windy conditions. The low top spinning draw is what is required at Miramar to combat the frequent unfavorable weather conditions.

The weather conditions that fronted the players on the first day was a cold southerly wind gusting up to 33 miles an hour in the afternoon. McDougall would struggle in these conditions and finish with a 79. He bounced back with a par round of 72 in the morning the following day in warmer conditions and a light northerly wind.

His total of 151 qualified him mid field in 17th position of the 32 qualifiers. Durry who is from Wellington and hence very familiar with these variable weather conditions top qualified with a very impressive score of 140.

It is customary in modern times in the NZ Amateur that the top qualifier plays the bottom qualifier in the first round of the match play. However in 1965 the top qualifier played the 17th qualifier. This meant Durry would play McDougall in the first round.

The report in the newspaper describes the match as follows;

For tension, the Durry v Ted McDougall match in the morning won hands down. Here was a match fit to rank as a final; the tragedy of it was that one player would have to lose. The Durry-McDougall match was a tremendous encounter. There was never more than one hole in it as first Durry then McDougall seemed to gain ascendancy. Durry three putted the 17th and McDougall stood on the 18th tee dormie one up.

Then lashed out at his tee shot and put it into the houses along Broadway. Durry, who could be forgiven for whistling 'Give my regards to Broadway' as the ball sped unerringly on its path, won the hole. McDougall sunk a great six foot pressure putt on the 19th to halve, but missed from 4ft. on the 20th and a great battle came to an end.

For anyone who has played the par-5 18th will appreciate, in a southerly wind, anything other than a well struck drive down the left side of the fairway away from the out of bounds is unlikely to stay in bounds. It is therefore imperative, especially for anyone who hits the ball with a fade, to line up to play to the adjourning fairway.

McDougall did appreciate this however he failed to execute. I mention this because there seems to have been an unwarranted negative response from all quarters of the media. Even John Hornabrook, winner of the 1939 NZ Amateur and Open, devoted more than half a page in his book *Goldern Years of New Zealand Golf* to this particular indiscretion on the part of McDougall.

Durry would go onto to win his second NZ Amateur title. Jones was beaten in the first round by D.K. Boone one of New Zealand's most under rated players. Also in the field was a very young John Lister. Ross Murray did not compete for business reasons.

Following the Amateur a six man New Zealand team was named to contest the Sloan Morpeth trophy against Australia on the Shirley Links golf course in Christchurch. The NZ team was made up of the four who competed in Rome plus John Means and Ian Woodbury who replaced Terry Leech who had to withdraw due to work commitments.

The interesting thing about this contest was that the format would consist of 36-holes of foursomes on the first day and then 36-holes of singles match play on the second day rather than the customary 18-hole matches in the past.

Australia as usual had a very strong team but it would be NZ who would gain the advantage after the completion of the foursomes.

The Australian pairing of Bell & Titheridge gave the New Zealand pairing of Means & Woodbury a hiding 9 and 7 but Jones and Murray overcame Crow and Hartley 2 and 1. It would be Durry and McDougall who would cause the big upset in beating the previously unbeaten, in all competitions, combination of Donohoe and Billings also by 2 and 1.

In the singles the following day Means would again struggle and by all accounts found the whole experience totally nerve racking going down to Bell 3 and 2. Woodbury bounced back from the heavy defeat the previous day to win his match against Titheridge 3 and 2.

Ross Murray lost his match to Donohoe 2 and 1 and with Durry halving his match against Hartley the Australians were well and truly back in the match.

McDougall was playing some brilliant golf against the Australian captain Phillip Billings and was five up at lunch. This was a 36-hole event however and with a combination of some poor play on the part of McDougall and Billings fighting back the match was all of sudden back to square with eight holes remaining. McDougall, fortunately for NZ, rediscovered his morning form and in the end had a comfortable 4 and 2 win.

At this point New Zealand were ahead 4.5 to 3.5. All New Zealand required now was at least a half from the remaining match between Jones and Crow. Jones who at one point held a six up advantage was having to fight off a major come back from Crow.

The match would effectively be determined on the 12th hole in the afternoon when Crow was looking likely to make birdie and get back to 2 down but Jones was having none of this and promptly holed out his 40 yard approach shot for an eagle. He had snuffed out Crow's comeback and held on to win 3 and 2.

The Sloan Morpeth Trophy was safely back in the New Zealand trophy cabinet.

After the Sloan Morpeth McDougall and the majority of the New Zealand team played in the 1965 NZ Open at the Auckland Golf Club located at Middlemore. The conditions were horrendous on the opening day and play had to be abandoned and all completed scores were discounted. They still managed 72-holes with two rounds played on the final day.

T. P. McLean wrote in the NZ Herald under the headline THOMSON TAKES RECORD 8TH GOLF OPEN. Precise Play Leaves Rivals Struggling.

Nobody else was fit to live on the same street as the great Australian P. W. Thomson when yesterday he won the New Zealand Open golf championship at Middlemore by the whopping margin of eight strokes.

Thomson scored 278, two under par for the 72-holes. Tied on second place with aggregates of 286 were another great Australian, K. D. G. Nagle who was runner-up in the United States Open this year, and the left-handed New Zealander R. J. Charles.

Two strokes behind followed the Englishman G. B. Wolstenholme, whose last round of 69 was one of five of the tournament to better par. On 291 were the Canterbury amateur R. C. Murray, whose final round of 67 was rewarded with the Jellicoe Cup as the lowest of the tournament, and also won the Bledisloe Cup for the leading amateur, and the Australian professional B. J. Coxon.

Another amateur the burly and powerful E. J. McDougall, shared the next place with the highly rated Australians J. Sullivan and E. A. Ball.

Results: New Zealand Open - November 1965 (Middlemore, Auckland)

1	P. W. Thomson (Victoria)	70	71	68	69	278
2=	R. J. Charles (New Zealand)	74	71	70	71	286
2=	K. D. G. Nagle (N.S.W)	70	72	71	73	286
4	G. B. Wolstenholme (UK)	74	73	72	69	288
5=	R. C. Murray* (Otago)	80	72	72	67	291

5=	B. J. Coxon (N.S.W.)	75	74	68	74	291
7=	**E. J. McDougall*(Tokoroa)**	**76**	**75**	**70**	**72**	**293**
7=	J Sullivan (South Australia)	71	76	73	73	293
7=	E. A. Ball (N.S.W.)	76	76	70	71	293
10	S. G. Jones* (Hastings)	75	71	77	73	296

At this juncture Ross Murray, Ted McDougall, Stuart Jones and John Durry would now be referred to as the 'big four' of New Zealand amateur golf - out of the same mold as John Hornabrook, Brian Silk, Bob Glading and Tim Woon who were the preeminent players pre and immediately post WWII during the so called *Golden Years of New Zealand Golf.*

The week following the NZ Open was the £1,000 Metalcraft sponsored tournament conducted at St Andrews in Hamilton. The majority of professionals from the Open would also play in this event. Charles and Nagle opted not to play however players such as Thomson, Wolstenholme, Roesink and other top Australians would play.

As this was the venue where McDougall had scored seven under par 281 to win the Waikato stroke play earlier in the year he also fancied his chances and decided to take more annual leave to play.

The event was played over 54 holes and it would be a dream start for McDougall as he shot rounds of 69 and 68 to lead P. W. Thomson and the South African C. Amm by two shots going into the final round.

Winston Hooper the Waikato journalist reported on the final day's play under the headline "McDougall's fourth-hole lapse left Thomson well in front".

There was something of an anti-climax when the Australian professional P. W. Thomson won the Metalcraft Industries Ltd, £1,000 golf tournament. Thomson won the event by three strokes but many left wondering just what would have happened had the Tokoroa amateur, E. J. McDougall, not blown up at the fourth hole in the final round.

At this-hole McDougall, the leader after both the first and second rounds, took a three over eight. In doing so he lost the great chance he had of heading a big field home and becoming the first amateur to perform such a feat since the golf circuit has been in operation.

This gave Thomson a big break on the rest of the field and the intense interest that had been building up about McDougall's chances of winning the event suddenly deflated.

Thomson went onto win with a score of 208, eight under par. Three strokes away in equal second were the professionals, R. R. Newdick, W. J. Godfrey of New Zealand and B. J. Coxon and A. A. Murray of Australia.

McDougall came in on 212, four behind Thomson, and had some compensation of being the top amateur.

There were two tournaments remaining on the NZ circuit before Christmas that McDougall would also compete.

At the £2,000 sponsored Caltex tournament at Paraparaumu McDougall scored 295 for an 11th place finish again won by Peter Thomson and in the final event of the year at the £2,000 NZ Forest Products sponsored event held on his home course Tokoroa McDougall shot seven under par 281 for a top 10 finish. Kel Nagle returned to New Zealand to win this event.

The 1966 season started where the 1965 finished off when at the Tauranga £2,000 pro-am McDougall finished 6th in the field with a score of 287. The event was won by Ross Newdick with a final round 64.

The NZ professional circuit was well established now and would continue to be supported by the top Australian players and several players from Britain, Holland and South Africa. The players who would regularly return season after season included, Peter Thomson, Kel Nagle, Bob Charles, Guy Wolstenholme and M. Roseink from Holland.

1966 was Eisenhower year. In New Zealand, and probably Australia as well, representing your country at the Eisenhower would undoubtable be the highlight of any amateurs playing career. New Zealand already had established a record to be proud of in this event and they would be looking to improve on their third place finish in Rome.

Heading into the 1966 season it was going to take something extraordinary from someone to force their way into the New Zealand team and replace any of the four who had competed in Rome. Jones had won the 1964 Amateur, and Durry the 1965 Amateur. Murray and McDougall had been the stand out players at the 1965 Freyberg Rose Bowl and they had also been the leading amateurs at the New Zealand Open finishing fifth equal and seventh equal respectively in a quality field.

The form of these four had been so convincing that Ian Wells, a leading golf journalist, would report;

Unless some younger golfer has an extraordinarily good run this year, it is safe to say that the New Zealand team for the Eisenhower Trophy already has picked itself.

The team, to be announced after the New Zealand amateur championship in September, seems certain to comprise the "big four" of New Zealand amateur golf -John Durry, Stuart Jones, Ted McDougall and Ross Murray.

The selection of the New Zealand team as outlined earlier was based on player performance at the interprovincial tournament for the Freyberg Rose Bowl Trophy, the New Zealand-Amateur, the North and South Island stroke play championships and the New Zealand Open.

McDougall had earned selection for the 1958 Eisenhower by virtue of winning the 1957 New Zealand Amateur and in 1964 he won the North Island stroke play championship to gain selection for Rome. He had also played consistently good golf in the other events considered for selection.

After playing an instrumental role, along with Ross Murray, in New Zealand finishing third at Rome he had continued to play some impressive golf. He had finished runner up in the 1964 New Zealand Amateur and capped off a very good season in 1965 with a top ten finish in the New Zealand Open.

All that remained to gain selection for Mexico were solid performances at the Freyberg played in May and the North Island stroke play to be played in August.

The NZ selectors however made the unprecedented decision to bring forward the New Zealand Amateur from its traditional November date to September and make it the final trial before selection. They also announced that selection would be based primarily on player form from May - being the Freyberg - through to the completion of the NZ Amateur in September.

This change in selection policy was problematic for McDougall. He had already decided he wasn't intending on playing in the New Zealand Amateur as it was to be played in Christchurch in the South Island which was a very expensive trip from Tokoroa in the heart of the North Island.

Secondly he was one of only very few players who had participated in both the 1964 and 1965 NZ Amateurs. He had therefore already competed in two NZ Amateurs since the Eisenhower in Rome. He didn't think he should have to play in a third one and considered his current form sufficient good enough to warrant selection.

The 1966 season started off well for Ted when he won the first trial for selection for the Waikato Freyberg team. He had rounds of 72 and 73 around the Lochiel course to head off Bruce Stevens by a shot.

In the Waikato Stroke Play McDougall had one bad round, an 81 in the second round as a consequence of taking a 10 on the fourth hole as two of his tee shots were last seen heading towards the Mighty Waikato River, but with three other good scores of 75, 71, and 73 still finished fourth on 300. Stuart Jones had crossed the border from Hawkes Bay and was the winner eleven shots ahead of Bruce Stevens who finished on 295.

McDougall was subsequently named No. 1 for Waikato to contest the Freyberg to be played at the Grange course in Auckland. Bruce Stevens was promoted from No. 4 in the previous year to No. 2.

In the Freyberg, Waikato finished second for the second successive year. Wellington won. McDougall had a mixed tournament. He had three convincing wins and two narrow 1-down losses to Durry and Leech and lost 3 and 1 to G. Lummis. Lummis also took down Stuart Jones on the final day.

Although only a fifty percent record, Ted was none the less happy with his over-all form. The media were impressed enough with the play of the 'big four' to go with the headline; 'Big Four' Impressive in First Major Golf Tournament.

Following the Freyberg McDougall helped his Tokoroa club win the Waikato Pennants. The report in Monday's local paper went under the headline McDougall Magnificent in Tokoroa Pennant Win

'MAGNIFICENT is the only word to describe the golf produced by Tokoroa's International star Ted McDougall, while leading his club to its second successive victory in the Waikato Pennant event which concluded at Tokoroa on Sunday.

After the first two rounds which were held at Waitomo, the home team held a four stroke advantage over Tokoroa. As a result of McDougall's amazing performance, and with steady support coming from his other team members, J. Page, D. Berry, J Winchester and D. Ryan, Tokoroa eventually won by only four strokes, in an intensely interesting finish.

The day however unquestionably belonged to McDougall who twice toured the par 72 layout in 66 strokes, which on his own admission represented the steadiest golf of his career.

He was in complete command throughout, requiring at the most a nine iron second shot to any par four hole. An early indication of what was to come was served by McDougall at the par four second when he placed his tee shot five feet from the pin, and holed the putt for an eagle two.

His next birdie came at the par five sixth, with a putt from four feet. He could be excused for his only mistake of the day when he required three putts from 25-feet on the recently cored surface.

Pars followed until the difficult 11th, which he birdied to move to three under the card. His next birdie came at the 16th with a ten foot putt-four under.

Playing now with the authority which has gained him the black blazer on so many occasions, he fired his tee shot down the left of the 18th fairway, and followed it up with the shot of a champion, a five wood four feet from the hole. The eagle putt went down for a score of 66.

He held the same respect for the first hole of his afternoon round (the 10th of the course) on which he followed a long drive with a two iron second 10-feet from the hole-two eagles in a row! A magnificent second to the 11th and an unerring six foot putt saw him card his second birdie on that hole, three under par after only two holes, and six under for his last five holes, each of which completed in three strokes.

His sequence was broken at the 12th at which he had to settle for a par four (missing a putt of 10-feet). Regulation threes followed at the 13th and 14th, whilst the 15th gave him his only long putt of the day, a curling 24-footer down the slope which never looked like missing.

For his last nine holes, this amazing golfer required only 28 strokes, against a par of 35!

His golf after that was copybook all the way with only two birdies-at the 9th (actual 18th) and 14th (actual 5th) of his round, although he putted for birdie on every other occasion!

The only unusual facet of this fantastic performance was that he scored only one two, and that on a par four hole.

Added to the two 66s McDougall recorded two rounds of 71 in the first round of the Pennant at Waitomo, giving him a four round total of 274, 14 under par. The closest to this score was Waitomo's T. Ormsby who was 22 strokes away on 296.

The other members of the Tokoroa team are to be congratulated on their steady play, in bringing the Pennant home for a second year.

Individual totals of the Tokoroa players are as follows: E. McDougall 274, J. Page 314, D Berry 309, J. Winchester (Waitomo only) 167, D. Ryan (Tokoroa only), 156, for a combined total of 1220.

Overall results: Tokoroa 1220 first; Waitomo 1224; Lochiel 1270 third.

McDougall then followed this up by winning the South Waikato match play title.

Ted went into the North Island stroke play full of confidence. He none the less put a lot of pressure on himself expecting he probably needed to win the event to gain national selection as he held firm on his decision not to play in the NZ Amateur.

As it transpired it would be Jones and Durry who would fight it out for the title with Jones on a score of 284 edging Durry by a single shot on the par-72 Te Awamutu layout.

McDougall had been playing well and was in contention heading into the final round after rounds of 72, 72, and 73. He however lost his composure in the final round when pushing too hard for a low score.

He had constant tree trouble and when he petulantly four putted the final green from 20-feet in front of the national selectors he probably didn't do himself any favors in signing for a 78 and a 5th equal placing on a score of 295. Bruce Stevens finished third on 290.

When Stuart Jones won his sixth New Zealand Amateur the following month McDougall still believed he had done enough to warrant selection for the Eisenhower team as no other player had played exceptional golf to oust any of the big four of New Zealand golf.

During the two year period since Rome; McDougall had finished runner-up in the 1964 NZ Amateur, lost in the first round to John Durry in the 1965 NZ Amateur, he had eight wins from twelve matches playing at No 1. for Waikato at the 1965 and 1966 Freyberg Rose Bowl, he had finished fifth equal in both the 1965 and 1966 North Island stroke play events and had been second amateur and seventh equal in the field at the 1965 NZ Open. He also had two wins against Australia for the Sloan Morpeth Trophy.

No player outside of Murray, Jones or Durry could match that consistent performance. The New Zealand selectors however had another agenda and named Bruce Stevens along with John Durry, Ross Murray and Stuart Jones to contest the Eisenhower in Mexico.

Jim Wallace, NZ's foremost golf journalist, came out in support of McDougall with the following headline -*McDougall's non-selection warrants an explanation …...McDougall's exclusion is one of the biggest 'boil overs' in recent golfing history and warrants an explanation. I suspect that McDougall was omitted because of his non-appearance at last week's national championships in Christchurch. If this is the case he has been harshly treated.*

The New Zealand team played Australia in their traditional pre-Eisenhower warm up event for the Sloan Morpeth Trophy played at the Manukau golf course in Auckland. Australia won 6-0.

The headlines were scathing:

No Ted, so NZ was trounced - *Associated Press*

NEW ZEALAND'S golf selectors must be asking themselves: "Why didn't we pick Ted McDougall?" after yesterday's pitiful performance against Australia in the Sloan Morpeth international at Manukau.

After two losses in the foursomes the singles results were as follows:

Donohoe beat Jones 8 and 7.

Billings beat Stevens 5 and 4

Berwick beat Durry 3 and 2

Hartley beat Murray 2 up

McDougall Missed in Stopping Golf Rout - *Jim Wallace*

New Zealand missed Ted McDougall, the finest short-iron player in the country, against Australia in the Sloan Morpeth at the weekend. If McDougall had been in the team instead of the out-of-form Stuart Jones or listless John Durry I am sure Australia would not have won 6-0.

....It is to be hoped McDougall will not be discouraged by being passed over this year. New Zealand golf badly needs him and it is regrettable he was not with the side when it left Auckland last night for Mexico City for the World Cup event next week.

When Will They Ever Learn - *the NINETEENTH wonders . . . .*

These are grim days in New Zealand golf-the days of the application of a means test to candidates for the national representative team to play in the world amateur teams' tournament for the Eisenhower Trophy at Mexico City next month.

The omission from the team of the burly big banger from Tokoroa, E. J. McDougall, can only be explained by his failure to compete in the national amateur championship tournament at Russley in Christchurch the other day. That failure was simply explained. As a married man with a family, McDougall couldn't afford to go to Christchurch. Which amounts to a means test.

It has happened before. When the team for the Eisenhower Trophy a year or two ago was under consideration, R. C. Murray, who was then of Christchurch, received loud and clear, a message that his selection depended upon his appearance in the North Island championship at Mount Denby, the highly attractive course at Whangarei. Murray also a family man with a young child, found it was not easy to part up with the £45 or thereabouts which the trip cost him.

He had the compensation of the trip to the tournament, but he smarted, as a good many of us, at the peremptory attitude of the selection committee. Their action was the less excusable because the Mt Denby, though justly celebrated for its beautiful timbering, was and remains a course not of the first class standard.

Before the championship at Russley, three past internationals, McDougall, J. P. Means and T. S. Leech, all announced that they could not afford to compete. This was regrettable. Any one, in fact all, of the three had a sufficient brilliance to knock off any contender in the field, "Emperor Jones" included. Their decision not to compete was, however, much more than regrettable: it was understandable.

This may be an Affluent Society, but not all of the members of it are partners in business or have extremely well-paid executive appointments. I would have thought the reaction to a bloke who said he couldn't afford to compete would be a certain sympathy.

I am not caviling at the selection of the Waikato No. 2, Bruce Stevens. He set his eye on the crest a few years ago. Since then, he has displayed total diligence. He has practised like the very devil, he has had ago at every possible tournament, he has won, deservedly, a reputation for being the most honest of triers and the even better reputation, also well deserved, of being a gentleman of the game.

One may suspect that his play is a little too well-mannered, that it would be stronger for a bit of naked power, but this cannot be proved until he steps into conflict on the long, mean, tough track on the Mexican heights.

The ways of sporting selectors are often unfathomable and here in golf is a case in point. At the beginning of the season the word passed quietly around that the Barron of Bridge Par, S. G. Jones himself was likely to be for the high jump. He might be the toughest competitor in New Zealand, as indeed, his efforts in the North Island at Te Awamutu and the national at Russley have unmistakable proved, but his record out of the country, especially in the medal tests of the Eisenhower, was, it was whispered, so indifferent as to justify his exclusion.

Amazingly enough, that record has been indifferent. With his tough, aggressive mind and outlook - both essential possessions to the top competitors in sport these days-he has terrorized scores of competitors in this country and turned them into a jangle of junior jerks. But, overseas, the "Emperor" hasn't had it; and an essentially nervous temperament which he mastered before he began to lord it over New Zealand golf has been, so it seems, a problem he has found baffling.

This is where the Terror of Tokoroa steps forward. He has had eight rounds in the Eisenhower Trophy, four at the inaugural tournament at St Andrews eight years ago and four more at Rome a couple of years ago. Seven of these rounds have counted in the New

Zealand total. This is a record far superior to Jones's record. It is a demonstration that, when the chips are down, McDougall has what it takes. This is the sort of man, surely, who is the answer to a selector's prayer.

Jones, of course, has long since put a stop to this silly talk that he was about to be heaved out on his ear. He keeps his ear as close to the ground as most people and when he, too, received the message, he reacted by pouring on the pressure and by firmly establishing himself as the best amateur golfer in the country. He simply could not be left out.

But neither, in my view, could McDougall, least of all because he could not afford to compete at Christchurch. What is a selection committee for? To strive, to seek, to find the right material to represent the country-surely this is it? And having found it, not to yield until something better comes along. Its purpose most decidedly is not to sit in judgment on competitors who for the time being haven't the wherewithal to compete.

You could throw a blanket over the number of first-class amateurs developed in New Zealand golf since the end of the Second World War. Robert Charles, Jones, Tim Woon (though he was coming along beforehand), Ross Newdick, Walter Godfrey, Ross Murray, John Durry - that's about the lot. And McDougall. Let's not forget. "We McDougall." Why then, having got him, let him go? As the song says, "When will they ever learn?"

The performance at the Eisenhower would be New Zealand's worst performance to date finishing eleventh. None of the New Zealand players broke 300. Murray and Stevens could hold their heads up high with solid four round totals of 301 but both Jones and Durry were again well off the pace.

Phillip Billings , who ironically McDougall had convincingly beaten in the Sloan Morpeth in 1965, would lead Australia to victory and it would be *Right Down the Blinking Middle* Shade of Great Britain and Ireland with a four round total of 283 who would be the stand out individual player of the tournament.

Mr. V. C. Hollis, of Cambridge, the convener of selectors would eventually explain his selection as follows:

"I refer critics to the selection panel's attitude toward form in the events between the Freyberg Rose Bowl-tournament early this season and the national amateur championships at Russley. Sufficient publicity was given to this intention.......the

selection was necessarily made on form during the period mentioned".

Although disappointed at missing selection McDougall did not dwell too long on his omission from the New Zealand team and was soon looking forward to his next tournament.

The NZ Forest Products sponsored event was to be played on McDougall's home course from the 8th -10th of December and would feature none other than Britain's Tony Jacklin. Also in the field would be P. W. Thomson, K. D. J. Nagle, R. J. Charles, G. B Wolstenholme, M. Roesink and a number of other high quality Australian players.

Unfortunately for McDougall about three weeks prior to the start of the event he had developed sciatica in his right leg. He was having treatment at Waikato hospital twice a week but had shown only a slight improvement. The advice to McDougall was he probably shouldn't be playing in this event.

In spite of being in obvious pain, when he gave a conducted tour of the course to the foreign players just prior to the event starting, he decided he would also play. It would not be a good experience. McDougall, who was most accustomed to scoring sub 70 rounds on his home course, would have rounds of 74, 73, 70, and limped home for a final round of 78 to finish well down the field. Things were not right and he was in obvious constant pain.

At the top of the leader board Tony Jacklin tied with Bob Charles for first place on 272. There would be no playoff. Guy Wolstenholme was third on 277. Special mention should be made of Peter Maude who was the leading amateur on 279 tied with Kel Nagle. Peter Thomson was a few more strokes back on 282. Tony Jacklin backed this result up by winning the NZ PGA played later that summer.

McDougall did not play in any of the professional events of the summer circuit whilst he continued to have treatment on his back. He still played some local golf however things would take a turn for the worse as reported in the press as follows:

E. J. McDougall, the Tokoroa, Waikato and former New Zealand representative golfer, who had hoped to win his way back to national consideration at the North Island tournament at Wanganui early next month has had his hopes shattered. He collapsed at his home last week with the recurrence of a back injury which troubled him late last year. He is now confined to bed in the Waikato Hospital, undergoing a two week course of treatment. He anticipates it may be several weeks before he is fully fit again.

Prior to the setback McDougall had shown fine form by creating a new course record of 66 at Tirau and he also had recent scores of 68 and 67 on his home course. McDougall represented New Zealand in Scotland in 1958 and in Italy in 1964. He said "I might try to win a place in the New Zealand team for Australia next year if all goes well"

It would be September 1967 before McDougall would be ready and fit enough to make his return to competitive golf.

Results: 1966 Eisenhower, Mexico

1. Australia

Phillip Billings	72	74	74	74	294
Harry Berwick	74	75	74	72	295
Kevin Donohoe	75	72	75	74	296
Kevin Hartley	68	78	77	73	296
Total	**214**	**221**	**223**	**219**	**877**

2. United States of America

Deane Beman	76	73	73	69	291
Robert Murphy	74	71	74	73	292
Ronald Gerrudo	76	73	74	74	297
A Downing Gray	76	80	73	75	304
Total	**226**	**217**	**220**	**216**	**879**

3. Great Britain and Ireland

Ronald D. B. M. Shade	74	69	72	68	283
Michael Bonallack	77	70	76	77	300
Gorden Cosh	77	76	75	73	301
Peter Townsend	77	79	84	76	316
Total	**228**	**215**	**223**	**217**	**883**

11. New Zealand

Ross Murray	75	73	75	78	301
Bruce Stevens	73	76	76	76	301
Stuart Jones	74	76	78	76	304
John Durry	78	75	81	78	312
Total	**222**	**224**	**229**	**230**	**905**

5 THE GREATEST AMATEUR IN THE WORLD

After spending three weeks in hospital undergoing tests McDougall then had to endure a month with his back in plaster. It was late July before he was fit enough to play some golf again at his home club.

In August he announced he was ready to play competitive golf again and he targeted the NZ Open as a tournament he would like to perform well in. The NZ Open was to be played at one of his favorite golf courses, St Andrews in Hamilton from the 15th to the 18th November.

His first tournament back from injury was the Tokoroa Open Day played on the 23rd of September where he scored 69 and 70. He was then invited to play for a Waikato 10 man team against Auckland in the inaugural 36-hole stroke play fixture. McDougall topped scored for Waikato with rounds of 70 and 69.

Auckland however beat Waikato by 1602 to 1621 with P. Vezich the top scorer for Auckland with rounds of 69 and 68 on the Waikare course.

McDougall then competed in and won his club championship beating E Bell 9 and 8 in the final and went on to score 67 and 72 in the Waikato champion of champions played on the Cambridge course to finish one stroke behind S. M. Leech.

The 1967/68 New Zealand summer professional circuit began on the 8th of November with a 36-hole pro-am event played at the Remuera course in Auckland sponsored by Skyline Homes.

McDougall gave a superb display of iron shots to card rounds of 68 and 66 for a three stroke victory.

Results: Skyline Homes Pro-am, Remuera, November 1967

1	**E. J. McDougall***	**68**	**66**	**134**
2=	F. Malloy	71	66	137
2=	J. Croskery	66	71	137
2=	F. X. Buckler	68	69	137
5	S. G. Jones*	69	70	139
6=	D. Machary	69	72	141
6=	T. C. Kendall	70	71	141
8=	D. Clark	72	70	142
8=	B. A. Stevens*	69	73	142
10	E. A. Southerden	69	75	144

*Amateur

This would be followed by a second placing to S. E. Reid in the Lochiel 54-hole invitation tournament with rounds of 72, 74 and 75.

The NZ Open was his next tournament. As usual it attracted a quality field including the likes of Peter Thomson, Kel Nagle, Bob Charles and Guy Wolstenholme.

The St Andrews links is considered one of New Zealand's finest golf courses and is situated on the western bank of the Waikato River just three miles from the city center.

K.D.G. Nagle dominated the event by virtue of a second round 64. He added rounds of two 70s and a 71 for a total score of 275. This was quite remarkable scoring as Jim Wallace would report -*brilliant golf was played through at times brilliant sun shine gale force winds and driving rain.*

It would however be McDougall's feat that would attract the headlines. The reporter A. M. Rowe would lead with -**McDougall (285) Is Top Amateur** and another would lead with -**McDougall's feat will long be remembered**

McDougall had finished fourth equal alongside Guy Wolstenholme.

McDougall, who was paired with Peter Thomson in the final round, outplayed Thomson 67 to 74. This would cause the five times Open Champion to comment afterwards -"*he is the best golfer in New Zealand at present, amateur or professional. His technique and attitude are strong features of his game*".

Results: 1967 New Zealand Open - St Andrews, Hamilton

1	K. D. G. Nagle (AUS)	70	64	70	71	275
2	E. A. Ball (AUS)	70	67	74	68	279
3	P. Townsend (UK)	67	70	72	71	280
4=	**E. J. McDougall***	**75**	**68**	**75**	**67**	**285**
4=	G. B. Wolstenholme (UK)	71	70	71	73	285
6	R. J. Charles	73	70	72	72	287
7	T. J. Woolbank (AUS)	68	74	72	74	288
8=	B. J. Coxon (AUS)	70	73	74	72	289
8=	S. J. Jones*	72	72	73	72	289
8=	J. D. Durry*	75	68	73	73	289
Also						
14	P. W. Thomson (AUS)	74	71	74	74	293
20	R. C. Murray*	72	72	76	74	294

There would be a break now until the Stars Travel $4,000 sponsored NZ PGA to be played at Mount Maunganui from the 4th of January 1968.

The NZ PGA at this time allowed amateurs into the field to add interest to the tournament. Amateur golf during the 1960s and forward into the 1970s received as much media coverage as the professional game.

Although Thomson, Nagle and Charles would be absent this year the field still included high caliber players such as E. W. Dunk, R. J. Shaw and R. J. Stanton all from Australia. Also returning would be Guy Wolstenholme from England and Martin Roesink from Holland along with New Zealand's best professionals including the likes of Dennis Clark, Walter Godfrey, Dennis Sullivan and John Lister to name a few.

McDougall played almost as well as he had done in the NZ Open. R. Shaw with a four round total of 278 edged out his fellow Australian countryman R. J. Stanton and NZs Walter Godfrey by a single shot. McDougall scored 283 to be leading amateur and finish sixth in the field.

There was however some controversy in the second round. There was some confusion concerning McDougall's tee time on the Friday of the second round. He had arrived at the course well in advance of his tee time, or what he thought was his tee time, and had been through his practice routine and headed to the first tee to find his group had already teed off and were already half way down the first fairway.

The organizing committee accepted some of the responsibility for the confusion and made the decision to allow McDougall to play at the back of the field with a marker rather than the usual disqualification for such a misdemeanor.

At the end of the round McDougall was about to sign for a 67, which would have placed him second after two rounds, but was told he had also been penalized two strokes.

McDougall protested the penalty on the grounds he should have been told before he teed off, which was some ninety minutes later after his scheduled tee time, unfortunately he lost his appeal and signed for a 69 instead.

Results: Stars Travel ($4000) NZPGA - Mt Maunganui - January 1968

1	R. J. Shaw (Tasmania)	69	69	71	69	278
2=	W. J. Godfrey	70	70	71	68	279

2=	J. Stanton (NSW)	72	67	70	70	279
4	E. W. Dunk (NSW)	72	67	68	73	280
5	G. B. Wolstenholme (England)	71	67	75	69	282
6	**E. J. McDougall***	**72**	**69**	**73**	**69**	**283**
7=	D. Clark	73	70	72	69	284
7=	H. R. Carver*	71	70	74	69	284
9	M. Gregson (England)	69	72	71	75	287
10	D. Sullivan	68	70	78	73	289

The final major event of the summer circuit was the $2,000 Spalding Masters. This was a 54-hole event played at the Tauranga course from the 8th to the 10th of January. As this was just a couple days after the completion of the PGA and in close proximity the field was essentially the same as for the NZ PGA.

John Lister set the pace with a six under par 64 and Martin Roesink finished with a scorching 63 but it was E. W. Dunk from NSW, Australia who would win with rounds of 65, 67 and 66 for a total of 198.

He finished just two strokes ahead of E. J. McDougall who played his most consistent golf to date with rounds of 68, 66, and 66 to total 200 and tie second with the PGA winner R. J. Shaw from Tasmania.

The journalist Winston Hooper made comparisons with Stuart Jones's effort in winning the 1965 Watties tournament in Hastings as an amateur. This was certainly McDougall's best performance in a major stroke play event and would go a long way in helping him achieve his ultimate goal of regaining his place in the New Zealand team.

Norman Von Nida, who was one of Australia's great golfers, and who was the current coach of the New Zealand team commented in his column for Sydney's Daily Telegraph -"*E. J. McDougall is playing about as well, if not better, than any amateur in the world today,*" said 'The Von'. "*He has been playing in all of the open tournaments this summer and has hardly been out of the top ten*"

Results: Spalding Masters ($2000) - Tauranga - January 1968

1	E. W. Dunk (NSW)	65	66	67	198
2=	**E. J. McDougall***	**68**	**66**	**66**	**200**
2=	R. J. Shaw (Tasmania)	69	67	64	200
4=	R. J. Stanton (NSW)	66	69	66	201
4=	M. Gregson (England)	70	66	65	201
6	J. M. Lister	64	68	71	203
7	W. J. Godfrey	66	72	66	204
8	M. Roesink (Holland)	72	71	63	206
9=	G. B. Wolstenholme (UK)	68	69	70	207
9=	T. C. Kendall	67	70	70	207

McDougall took a couple of weeks off before competing in the Morrinsville 72-hole Waikato amateur event. He opened with a 62 to break his own course record of 63 and follow this up with rounds of 65, 71 and 70 to total 268 for a very comfortable win on this par 69 course.

He then followed this up by winning the locally sponsored Nihill pro-am which featured some of New Zealand's best resident professionals with scores of 70, 71, and 66 on his home course.

Jim Wallace, perhaps New Zealand's foremost golf writer in this era, wrote a feature article on McDougall on his come back from his enforced lay-off. He began his column by referring back to St Andrews, Scotland in 1958 on the wind and rain swept course when Bobby Jones congratulated McDougall on his magnificent 72 and he would utter "*That was a great round - one of the finest by any standards*".

Wallace wrote about McDougall's achievement over the summer but also commented -*The long layoff allowed the 30 year clerk to consider his game and when he played his first round after leaving hospital, he found the layoff was, in fact of some value* - he went on to comment - *McDougall now has his sights set on Melbourne in October for the world amateur series and the Eisenhower Cup.*

73

The journalist Ian Wells followed up with another feature article based on information he received from Mr. Derek Welsh who kept the handicap records for the Tokoroa Golf Club.

The headline read…**"MR BIG" of New Zealand golf is producing the figures to threaten amateur leaders anywhere: 5865/84=69.82.**

It's the equation of the year and it has been set by a 30 year old, 19-stone colossus who seems bent on making a mockery of golf mathematics in this country. Striking out boldly on the comeback trail to international selection, Ted McDougall who grips the golf club and wields a wedge with finesse of an artist putting the finishing touches to a color painting, is chasing the silver fern leaf by establishing scoring feats that may never be surpassed in New Zealand golf.

In a period of nearly 12 months to the end of January, this mighty golfer amassed a scoring record of incredible proportions. For his 84 rounds, he had taken 5,865 strokes- and one doesn't need to be an Einstein to arrive at an average of 69.82 strokes per round.

My own initial reaction to these figures was one bordering on total disbelief but a quick call to the Tokoroa Golf Club handicapper, Derek Welsh confirmed them. Mr. Welsh, a note of understandable pride in his voice, also pointed out that 30 of McDougall's 84 rounds were under 70 strokes and that the average score for his last 25 rounds was 68.44!

While the courses in the United States are obviously very different from those in New Zealand, it is possible to draw some comparisons with scoring there. Arnold Palmer won the Vardon Trophy for scoring last year with an average of 70.188 for 85 rounds. The winner in the States usually averages 70 point something and the last time 70 was broken was in 1961 when Palmer recorded 69.859.

It is not as if McDougall's average has been helped by the conditions. His 84 rounds stretch over a virtual 12-month period and, in any case, leading golfers do not receive too much assistance from summer conditions in this country. What they gain on fairway run is often offset by hard ground which makes approach work somewhat tricky.

McDougall makes a point of putting in the card for every round he plays, a factor which ensures a true handicap. His handicap has gone from two to plus-two and has achieved this by returning cards from as many other courses as he has from his home course at Tokoroa, where he is the club's vice- captain.

This is the true test of a golfer's handicap and I have always believed that New Zealand should have a national handicaps as well as club handicaps. This would mean that a player would have to return cards from a number of different courses to obtain a national handicap and would also ensure a truer handicap system. This method is enforce in Australia, where there are State as well as club handicaps. There are many one and two handicap golfers in New Zealand who are virtually reduced to six or seven handicappers when playing away from their own course.

In my book Ted McDougall is a certainty for the New Zealand team for the Eisenhower Trophy at Melbourne in October. In fact he would be my first choice. The McDougall skill is unchallenged but it is interesting to note that two of the greatest figures, Peter Thomson and Norman von Nida, recently singled out the big man for special praise.

Thomson after playing the final round of last year's New Zealand Open with McDougall, told me that "he is the best golfer in New Zealand at present, amateur or professional. His technique and attitude are strong features of his game." Von Nida, who spent time in New Zealand several months ago conducting a Wills coaching school, showered a bouquet or two McDougall's way in the column he writes for Sydney's Daily Telegraph.

"E. J. McDougall is playing about as well, if not better, than any amateur in the world today, "said "The Von". He has been playing in all the open tournaments this summer and has hardly been out of the top ten".

McDougall after more than 18 months away from serious golf, started playing in earnest last October. Every weekend since then, the giant New Zealand Forest Products credit supervisor has been out on the course playing and practising. The one let-off he expects to have this year is at Easter when he hopes to take his wife to Taupo for a holiday-the holiday being the first prize he won as top amateur in the N.Z.P.G.A. Stars Travel championship at Mt Maunganui in January.

He first played for New Zealand in 1958. "I did not think I was a particularly great golfer then," he confesses. His one disappointment in golf occurred in 1966. "I had won back my place in the New Zealand team for the Eisenhower Tournament in Rome in 1964 and was disappointed to miss selection for Mexico in 1966." he says. "One round in the North Island-a 78 cost me the chance".

"I would not say I am hitting the ball better than before but I am using my head more now. I am a stroke player, not a match player, and I play the course all the time.

Nowadays I play safe and my worst round for a very long time is a 75. At Tauranga in the Spalding Masters, I made only one mistake in the whole tournament and it cost me the chance of winning. In the first round needing two fours for a 66 and feeling elated, I over clubbed at the 17th and took a six for a round of 68. I followed with two 66s to end up on 200, two strokes behind Bill Dunk, who won the event".

McDougall's superb effort at Tauranga came a couple of days after he had finished top amateur in the P.G.A. at Mt Maunganui. He had rounds there of 72,69,73,69 for 283 to trail the winner Bob Shaw, by five strokes. A few weeks later, he spread-eagled the field in the tournament at Morrinsville with a course record opening round of 62, a second round of 65 and final rounds of 71 and 70 for a total 268. "I have been hitting a high percentage of greens in recent months and getting a few putts in," big Mac tells me. "My putting has never been the strongest feature of my game but its improving."

6 MELBOURNE 1968

Immediately prior to the start of the 1968 Freyberg to be played in May it appeared as though the New Zealand team for the Eisenhower would be Ted McDougall, Stuart Jones, John Durry and Ross Murray.

This would be one of the most experienced teams entered. McDougall, Jones and Durry, along with Bob Charles, comprised the team in the first Eisenhower in Scotland as far back as ten years ago!

The New Zealand team however would not be named until after the Freyberg Rosebowl had been played and the final trial for selection would be the North Island stroke play championship.

McDougall would top qualify along with Trevor Ormsby in the Waikato trials played over six rounds. It would however be on the opening day of the Waikato pennant series that McDougall produced his best golf with rounds of 70 and a course record equaling 63 on his home track to assist in giving the Tokoroa club an early commanding 23 stroke lead over the other 14 clubs competing.

McDougall was named number one for Waikato to contest the Freyberg Rose Bowl inter provincial tournament to be played at New Plymouth.

He maintained his form leading into the Freyberg and would be four under par in beating Ross Murray 3 and 2 in a practice round. T. P. McLean would report that the Waikato team led by McDougall, the Hawkes Bay team led by Jones and the Canterbury team led by Murray were the favorite

77

teams to win the event and not the defending champions Auckland.

The number of teams who contested for the Freyberg Rose Bowl had now increased from 12 to 15 provinces and the team size reduced from six to five to allow for the growth. Also the event was now played over seven rounds rather than the previous six.

Waikato dominated over the first four rounds with four convincing wins. The key match for Waikato would be against Hawkes Bay in the fifth round and McDougall would be up against Stuart Jones. The match would not disappoint for tension and emotion. The outcome would come down to the final hole in the match between Jones and McDougall. Playing the last hole the match was all square which is what Waikato needed for a 3-2 win.

Jones was safely on the green in regulation two however McDougall was bunkered. He then produced a brilliant recovery stroke to within one and half feet. Jones missed his birdie attempt and McDougall had secured the vital half Waikato needed for the win. Jones was moved to comment after the match -"*Year by year Ted McDougall is growing greater and greater as a golfer.*"

It was a very emotional McDougall who walked off the 18th green after getting the crucial half against Jones. He had set Waikato up nicely to launch their final assault on Otago and Auckland in the final two rounds.

Waikato were convincing winners over Otago in the morning to virtually secure the Freyberg Rose Bowl for the first time. There was a slim chance that Taranaki could win but only if Waikato were to be beaten 5-0 by Auckland and only if Taranaki could win their final match against Bay of Plenty also by 5-0. Neither would eventuate.

Against Auckland McDougall defeated B. P. Vezich 6 and 5. The match ended with McDougall almost driving the 365 yard 13th and he then proceeded to chip in for an eagle two. Waikato's number two Graham Stevenson halved with B. Rafferty, the number 3 Trevor Ormsby won 6 and 5 against Ken Hankin and Keith Haggie and Peter Maude also record wins over Wilkinson and Stevens.

Waikato had finished the tournament with a perfect seven straight wins and an impressive 28.5 out of 35 individual matches.

Taranaki, Hawkes Bay and Auckland finished on five wins. McDougall was unbeaten for the tournament with five wins and two halves and was named player of the tournament.

The final event before the selection of the New Zealand team to compete for the Eisenhower trophy was the North Island championship played at the Waitomo course on August 24-25. It would be 1964 all over again.

Ross Murray was again summoned by the national selectors to make an appearance and John Durry, who had missed the Freyberg Rose Bowl for health reasons, was also required to play. There would again be controversy, this time concerning Stuart Jones.

Whilst New Zealand had competed in the 1967 Commonwealth tournament in Canada they had also played in the Canadian Amateur championship which Jones won. It was now 1968 and Jones wanted to return and defend his title, however, it clashed with the North Island stroke play. The New Zealand selectors were very reluctant for Jones to play in Canada and preferred he stay in New Zealand and compete in the North Island stroke play. Jones however insisted on defending his Canadian Amateur title and paid his own expenses to Canada.

In the meantime McDougall continued on with his very good form and won comfortably with a four round total of 287 to finish four shots ahead of Ross Murray just as had happened in 1964.

John Durry had a reasonable tournament with three good scores but finished with a 79 and an overall eleventh placing. Bruce Stevens who had played in Mexico had a steady tournament to finish fourth equal.

Results: 1968 North Island Stroke Play Championship - Waitomo

1	E. J. McDougall (Tokoroa)	74	73	69	71	287
2	R. C. Murray (Temuka)	75	74	72	70	291
3	P. A. Maude (Waitomo)	71	73	73	77	294
4=	G. R. Lummis (Nelson)	79	76	70	71	296

4=	P. K. Cleland (Manukau)	71	75	77	73	296
4=	T. Ormsby (Waitomo)	73	76	73	74	296
4=	B. A. Stevens (Titirangi)	75	71	76	74	296
4=	P. Garner (Grange)	71	72	75	78	296
9=	M. Hall (Waitomo)	76	76	72	73	297
9=	K. B. Haggie (Te Aroha)	76	75	74	72	297
11	J. D. Durry (Paraparaumu)	73	72	74	79	298

The New Zealand team was duly named immediately after the completion of the tournament and this time there was no Stuart Jones. The team was McDougall, Murray, Durry and Stevens. Jones was disappointed to miss selection however he did comment -"*I have had a wonderful run. The team chosen is a very good one and I think they will do very well in Melbourne*"

The Eisenhower was scheduled to be played from October 9 to 12.The only serious golf the New Zealand team had played since the completion of the Freyberg Rose Bowl in May and the onset of winter had been the North Island stroke play at the end of August.

It was therefore imperative that the team get some serious competition prior to the Melbourne event starting. New Zealand had been scheduled to play Australia for the Sloan Morpeth trophy in Sydney on the first of October however Australia pulled out at the last moment.

There was also the possibility of playing in the New South Wales open in late September however this also fell through. Instead they played a Wellington selection team at Miramar in horrendous conditions just prior to leaving for Melbourne. This was a totally unsatisfactory build up to a major tournament where there were high expectations for a top performance.

Norman von Nida had been talking up New Zealand's chances of success and the general feeling amongst many of the players competing was New Zealand had shown the best form and appeared very confident at the end of the three days of practice rounds on the 6,946 yard par 73 composite course.

The New Zealand team also had support from its 300 plus supporters who had made the three and half hour flight across the Tasman Sea.

New Zealand opened with a solid score of 224 made up of rounds of 74 from Stevens and a pair of 75s from McDougall and Murray. This placed them in a handy fifth position at the conclusion of day one.

Australia made the early running with 216 led by a 68 from K. Donohoe. It was reported that the NZ team had many opportunities for a better score but all had struggled on the very fast Royal Melbourne greens. McDougall, who was particularly unhappy with his putting, went as far as to change his putter for the second round.

The NZ team scoring improved by a single stroke in the second round with a pair of 74s from Stevens and Murray and a pair of 75s from McDougall and Durry. They would however drop to seventh position as the American team made a charge with scores of 68 from M. Giles III and 69 from R Siderowf.

McDougall had a great opportunity for a sub-par round when he stood on the 17th tee at even par. He absolutely boomed a drive down the middle of the 526 yard par 5-hole and he was only thinking one option when he prepared to play his second shot and it wasn't laying up.

He struck a very nice three wood heading to the left side of the green. Unfortunately after it landed, a yard on the right side of one of the three bunkers protecting the green, the ball took a hard kick to the left and finished in the bunker.

He then proceeded to thin the long bunker shot through the back of the green and would eventually finish with a seven. He pared the last for a two over 75.

McDougall received a fair amount of criticism from his supporters and two of the NZ Council representatives suggested McDougall should have played safe on the 17th by playing short of the bunkers that protected the green. Norman von Nida however supported his decision, "*McDougall played the right shot.*" He said. "*The only way to beat this course is by attacking it. There was only a foot between it being a great shot and a disastrous one.*"

New Zealand again scored 223 on day three to hold onto seventh position. Murray scored a fine 72. The Great Britain and & Ireland team took a commanding lead into the final round after a superb 66 from Michael Bonallack. He was backed up with very good scoring from Shade (70), Cosh (71), and Oosterhuis the non-counting score of 72. They had a seven shot lead heading into the final round over the United States. Australia was a further thirteen back in third position.

Great Britain and Ireland however struggled in the difficult conditions they encountered on the final day. Shade was a very disconsolate man after he missed a seven foot putt on the final green that would have forced a playoff with America.

Canada edged passed Australia for third. New Zealand had the third best total on the final day but could not improve on seventh place.

It was a disappointing end to the tournament for the New Zealand team and their large contingent of supporters. On a positive note Ross Murray finished eighth in the individual standings.

No-one in the team had a particularly bad tournament. The damage was done in the second and third rounds when someone in the team needed to score low to keep pace with the United States and Great Britain & Ireland teams but were unable to do so.

Australia must have also been disappointed with their fourth place finish after leading on day one on their home track.

It is difficult to understand why the New Zealand administrators could not have organized a better preparation for the team after Australia pulled out of the Sloan Morpeth Trophy.

Had the New Zealand team been able to play in an event in Australia prior to the start of the tournament I have no doubt their performance would have been much improved.

Results: 1968 Eisenhower, Royal Melbourne, Australia

1. United States of America

Marvin Giles, III	74	68	71	73	286
Richard L. Siderowf	74	69	73	73	289
Jack W. Lewis, Jr	72	74	72	78	296
Bruce Fleisher	77	76	73	75	301
Total	**220**	**211**	**216**	**221**	**868**

2. Great Britain and Ireland

Michael Bonallack	72	72	66	76	286
Peter Oosterhuis	70	71	72	76	289
Ronald D. B. M. Shade	76	72	70	77	295
Gordon Cosh	79	74	71	79	303
Total	**218**	**215**	**207**	**229**	**869**

3. Canada

Gary Cowan	73	69	72	79	293
Robert L. Wylie	78	73	71	76	298
Jim Doyle	79	73	79	71	302
John Johnston	74	75	80	76	305
Total	**225**	**215**	**222**	**223**	**885**

7. New Zealand

Ross Murray	75	74	72	73	294
Bruce Stevens	74	74	76	77	301
Ted McDougall	75	75	77	75	302
John Durry	76	75	75	79	305
Total	**224**	**223**	**223**	**225**	**895**

Although the Eisenhower had been a personal disappointment for McDougall his personality is such that he doesn't dwell too long on a poor round or tournament and allow himself to fall into the trap of over analyzing his game.

A week after his return to New Zealand he immediately won the Waikato Champion of Champions with rounds of 71 and 67 at the Waikare course.

The New Zealand amateur was played soon after at Titirangi in Auckland and whilst McDougall lost in the first round to G. K. McKinnon he qualified equal third with Stuart Jones with rounds of 71 and 74.

Bruce Stevens finally broke the Jones/Durry domination since 1961 to win on his home track and vindicate his selection for New Zealand in the previous two Eisenhower's.

McDougall round out the year by playing in two exhibition matches. The first was played at Balmacewen in Dunedin, Otago. The Otago Golf is the oldest club in New Zealand and was established in 1892. There had not been a lot of top-flight golf played here for some time and so the club captain Mr. Alex Gardner took it upon himself to organize a four ball match to be sponsored by his company Gardner Motors. There would be $300 up for grabs to the professional of the winning team and an appropriate trophy for the winning amateur. The course proceeds would go to Crippled Children Society and the Intellectually Handicapped Society.

Mr. Jim Scouler, whilst he was in Australia with the New Zealand team, organized Ted McDougall to play with Walter Godfrey and Ross Murray would partner the resident professional Alistair Kidd.

Murray and Kidd had been unbeaten on their four previous occasions in similar type matches. They took an early lead when Murray birdied the third however Godfrey immediately birdied the next to put them back on level terms.

There was little to separate the two combinations until the middle stages of the second nine were reached and McDougall played the most telling of the day-a mighty drive at the 276-yard thirteenth, which found the front of the green and gave him a birdie. It brought the breakthrough each team was endeavoring to find.

Three holes later the Tokoroa amateur scored his second birdie of the match with a two at the short sixteenth to put his team dormie two up. The breakthrough was then complete. All four players carded fours on the final hole of the match to provide a fitting climax to what had been always a close and often exciting match. For the record Godfrey carded 69 and McDougall 71.

At the prize giving ceremony, the Mayor, Mr. J. G. Barnes, congratulated the players on the fine exhibition they had given and also thanked the sponsoring company not only for bringing four of New Zealand's leading golfers together but also the contributions it was making to two worthy organizations.

McDougall was then invited to play in another exhibition match with Miss Marilynn Smith, one of the leading stars of the United States women's circuit.

Winston Hooper would report on the exhibition played at the Lochiel Golf Club in the Waikato.

Tokoroa's New Amateur golf representative, E. J. McDougall, arrived to play in Saturday's exhibition match golf match at Lochiel with big doubts about his form. He hadn't been playing much golf and his plans to visit Lochiel for just one practice during last week had been thwarted at the last moment.

It was on his mind that he would have to play right up to form to match the three famed companions, Miss Marilynn Smith, one of the leading stars of the US professional circuit, Glennis Taylor, the New Zealand woman's representative, and the genial Lochiel professional, F. X. Buckler.

And when he drove deep into the trees on the left on the second hole his confidence wasn't exactly boosted.

But, as it transpired he needn't have worried for he turned out to be the star of day making six birdies in carding a four under 68. This was with an assessment of a five on the par four second when he picked up after his partner, Miss Smith, had been near the pin for two.

Buckler was round in a steady 72, Miss Smith, the first time she had played the course, in 74 and Miss Taylor 75 with one hole out. For the record books McDougall and

Smith won 4 and 3.

A gallery of up to 750 watched the players hit off. A great 40-foot putt on the long third for a birdie four by Miss Smith seemed to spur the others to greater deeds after a quiet start. Miss Smith, Buckler and McDougall hit splendidly to the fourth green. All finished within eight feet of the hole, but only McDougall clinched the birdie.

All four were putting for birdies at the fifth, none eventuated, while McDougall, after having to hit through a maze of trees, scrambled a five on the seventh. The others had fours.

McDougall's second birdie came at the eight when his delicate chip from just off the front of the green finished two foot from the pin. It was Buckler's turn to shine at the ninth when a perfectly played wedge stopped a mere 12 inches from the cup.

McDougall drove the 10th green making full use of the wind and run. He made the expected birdie. Miss Smith sank another long putt ("the best I've done in New Zealand") for her second birdie. McDougall's drive at the 11th was down the sixth fairway, but his recovery was so brilliant that his putt for a birdie was only three feet. He sank a 15-footer for his third successive birdie at the 12th and had his birdie putt dropped at the 13th he would have really opened out at the remaining holes. "If that putt had've dropped, I would have been right," he said later.

Misses Smith and Taylor saw their birdie putts do everything but drop at the 13th. Miss Taylor and McDougall had regulation fours at the 14th and Miss Smith and Buckler fives. McDougall was the only one on the par three 15th for an easy three, while Misses Smith and Taylor chipped close enough for their pars.

Miss Smith, Buckler and McDougall, who found his ball mysteriously sitting on a wooden tee in the middle of the fairway, all had fours at the 16th. Buckler, at last, saw one of his longer putts drop for a birdie on the 17th and Miss Smith, Buckler and McDougall finished with a flourish with birdie fours at the eighteenth".

7 MADRID 1970

The 1969 season started with the Nihill sponsored event at Ted's home course. He shot a pair of 69s to head off Stuart Jones who had a pair of 72s. They attracted a small gallery in the afternoon which was noticeable for its keen but friendly rivalry. McDougall also drove the 367 yard ninth hole.

The Waikato stroke play was played in early April at St Andrews as the final trial for the selection of the five man Freyberg Rose Bowl team. McDougall with a score of 287 won the event by 16 strokes from Ormsby and McNabb on 303 played in testing windy conditions.

The Waikato team only had two players remaining from the winning 1968 team. Bruce Stevens also had moved north to Titirangi. The Waikato team had a youthful look with Houltham, Reid and Bryant coming in to compliment Ormsby and McDougall.

Waikato were the defending champions however it was the Wellington team made up of Durry, Rafferty, Woodbury, Barltrop and Lacy who were the hot favorites.

Wellington halved with Hawkes Bay in the second round and then again with Manawatu-Wanganui in the fourth. They then won every other game convincingly. Hawkes Bay however won all their remaining games after their half with Wellington and took out the Freyberg Rose Bowl.

The key match for Hawkes Bay occurred against Otago in the sixth round when three of the Otago players had short putts on the final green to deny

Hawkes Bay victory but they all were unable to convert their putts to deny Hawkes Bay victory.

Waikato finished mid field with its young inexperienced team however McDougall personally had a good tournament including beating Stuart Jones from Hawkes Bay 2 and 1.

Following the Freyberg McDougall led his Tokoroa team to victory in the Waikato pennant series with two rounds of 68 on the par 70 Te Aroha golf course.

He would then lose 5 and 4 to Jones in the annual Hawkes Bay v Waikato match held at Waiohiki, Napier.

Next on the agenda was the North Island championship to be played at the Hokowhitu course in Palmerston North from May 31st through to June 2nd. In the past this event had been a four round stroke play event held over the weekend however the New Zealand Golf Council, in its infinite wisdom, decided to make this a match play event for this particular year.

When you consider New Zealand did not have a national stroke play event during this period, the North Island and South Island events were in effect the de-facto NZ stroke play events hence it is difficult to understand the rationale for making this a match play event when there were already ample match play events around the country to judge a player's match play temperament.

A New Zealand team was to be named at the completion of this event to play Australia later in the year at Royal Adelaide. There was a very good field assembled and at the completion of 36-holes of qualifying Durry held a one stroke lead over Murray with McDougall in third place alongside Rafferty.

Rodney Barltrop, Jones and Stevens were also in touch with the leaders.

It is unfortunate that there couldn't have been a fitting climax as it turned into a convoluted match play event with only 16 players qualifying in the top group and first round losers then required to play in another competition with some matches not completed due to darkness, not surprising as it was now winter! The event turned into a farce. For the record Murray beat Jones 3 and 2 in the final.

McDougall was named in the eight man team to play Australia. According to media reports he was fortunate to be included because of his perceived poor form in Melbourne and at the North Island championship where he lost in the first round.

Australia won narrowly 7-5. The damage for NZ was done in the foursomes played over 36-holes on the first day. McDougall and Brown had won 7 and 5 over Mackay and Toogood in very difficult conditions, being a howling northerly, however the other three pairings all lost their matches.

New Zealand fought back on day two halving the singles 4 all. McDougall won his match 2up against Mackay.

Brown also had another win against Toogood. Clarke beat Burgess, Rafferty beat Hartley, Jones lost to Gale, Durry lost to Jack Newton and Murray lost to Donohoe.

Although this was not the result New Zealand had hoped for it was none the less a reasonable performance on Australian soil and had been a particularly satisfying result for McDougall again recording two wins.

The headline he returned home to was-**McDougall Has Answered His Critics.**

The following week he came home in 29 for a 67 in the Saturday scramble at his home club and the following day he won the Tokoroa Open with rounds of 71 and 69.

Whilst McDougall was in Adelaide it was reported in the press that Billy Casper was visiting New Zealand in October and he had requested to play in an exhibition match with two amateurs and a professional. It was likely that McDougall would be one of the invited amateurs.

Billy Casper had won the US Open in 1959 and 1966 and was one of the most prolific winners on the US PGA tour during the 1960s. In 1966 he converted to the LDS Church. He was in New Zealand visiting fellow Mormons in Hamilton.

The Mormon temple in Hamilton was the first temple of The Church of Jesus Christ of Latter-day Saints to be built in the southern Hemisphere.

The press reported -*Casper's sincere, dedicated approach to his livelihood and to life is obvious within moments of meeting him. - He feels that his religion has a made a better golfer of him.*

There were two rounds played at the Lochiel course in Hamilton featuring John Lister as the invited professional and Bruce Rafferty the other amateur alongside McDougall.

On the Friday the players were confronted with heavy rain and a wet course however this did not prevent a huge crowd from turning up to watch some fine golf being played in the horrible conditions. Lister was the star of the first day scoring a two under 70. Casper had a 71 and Rafferty and McDougall respectable 73s.

T. P. McLean reported on the exhibition in the NZ Herald -*Casper had kind words for his companions. He thought Lister extremely promising and good enough, with experience, to make a sufficient showing on 'the tour' - the American professional circuit of 45 tournaments for which Lister next month hopes to qualify.*

Casper considered McDougall the best of the three at striking the ball and was sympathetic about, and a little astonished by, the inability by the man to tie all the loose ends together, particularly on the putting green.

Casper considered Rafferty's swing to be a little stiff and angular-and in truth more than one was hit off line-but he was greatly impressed by the young man's evident determination, especially on the green.

On the Saturday Casper shot 71, Rafferty 74 and Lister and McDougall 75s. The following April Casper won the US Masters.

The NZ Amateur was played in Nelson and attracted a quality field including two Australians Alan Snape and Rod White, who had moved to NZ three years earlier, they would take out the foursomes with an impressive score of 142.

This score had only been bettered once in the history of the tournament. McDougall and Stevens finished second on 145 and they would share top honors in the qualifying rounds with both players scoring consecutive 71s.

T. P. McLean was again reporting on the event and described some of McDougall's play in the second qualifying round as follows -*The contest of the two leaders looked likely to end as early as the fourth hole when a sliced tee shot by McDougall into what seemed to be completely open ground disappeared forever. The unfortunate man fumed his way back to the tee to play another, and fumed his way back to a double bogey 6. He took another 6 at the 570-yard sixth hole and thus was three over the card. Then he put childish things behind by scoring four successive 3s, three of them for birdies. He had a 4 at the 11th for another birdie.*

There were a number of upsets on the opening day of match play when R. C. Murray, B. A. Stevens the defending champion, and S. G. Jones were all eliminated. McDougall won both his games comfortably but would face tougher competition in the third round in the form of Alan Snape.

Graeme Stevenson, McDougall's Waikato team mate, had defeated an in form Graeme Lummis in the second round after he had eliminated Jones in the first round. He then faced Bruce Rafferty in the third round.

It would be the two Waikato team mates who would win their way through their quarter final and semi-final matches to meet in a David versus Goliath final. After cold and grey weather in the morning the sun would break out in the afternoon which attracted a crowd of over 800 to watch the final.

Jim Wallace would report -*The underdog, Graham Stevenson, of the Waikato club at Te Kauwhata, produced an exhibition of fine golf to win the NZ Amateur title. In a match which at times produced golf to match the best ever seen in amateur finals and, at other times, golf of a mediocre standard, Stevenson beat his Waikato team-mate Ted McDougall two and one in the 36-hole event.*

Following the Amateur Ted played in a number of professional events over the summer. The highlight was winning the 18-hole $1,500 pro-am event held at the Te Puke course as part of the West Bay Festival of Golf.

The significance of the event was the quality of the field. McDougall shot a seven under par 66 and tied with Peter Thomson, John Lister and Glen McCully from Australia. Also in the field were Maurice Bembridge, Guy Wolstenholme, David Graham and Graham Marsh.

McDougall also played well in the NZ PGA played at Mt Maunganui from January 9 to 11. He finished with a disappointing 1 over par 74 for a combined score of 9 under par 283 on the par 73 course. He finished 1 shot behind Stuart Jones to be 2nd amateur in the field. The tournament was won by K. D. G. Nagle on 268 with John Lister in second place on 271.

On February the 20th McDougall was invited along with Stuart Jones, Bruce Stevens and Graham Stevenson to play an exhibition match to open the newly created Wairakei resort course just north of Taupo. The Minister of Tourism, Mr. Walker, officially declared the now best course in New Zealand open.

The 1970 Freyberg Rose Bowl was next on the agenda for McDougall. The trials for selection of the Waikato team typically consisted of eight rounds of accumulated stableford points played off scratch. McDougall led the scoring with a total of 287 stableford points.

He was subsequently selected number one for the Waikato team in the lead up matches to the Freyberg. There was some controversy however when Graham Stevenson was selected ahead of McDougall for the Freyberg to be played in Invercargill.

The convener of selectors announced that the move was more about acknowledging Stevenson as the national champion rather than this being about dropping McDougall to No. 2. McDougall had played well in the lead up matches and the journalist Owen Cook would report -*Much more serious for McDougall, however, is the influence of his number two placing on his chance of representing New Zealand at the Eisenhower trophy in Spain later this year. It is well known that the national selectors will be looking closely at the form of the top players at the Freyberg event and it will be difficult to assess McDougall against the second strings.*

The Freyberg was played at the earlier date of March 18th - 21st at Otatara in Invercargill. Waikato had a reasonable tournament with 5 points and 19.5 games to finish fourth. McDougall won 6 of his 7 matches in the number two spot. Stevenson found the going tough in the No. 1 spot and recorded only 1 win in his seven matches. Auckland took out the title with 6.5 points from a possible 7.

Following the Freyberg McDougall recorded his third win in the Waikato stroke play played over Easter weekend. In front of one of the national selectors he had four consistent rounds of 72,71,71,73 to win by four from Paul Shadlock.

He was then selected at number one to play Hawkes Bay in their annual fixture to be played at Tokoroa. Ted was five under the card in beating the *emperor* Stuart Jones 3 and 2.

All that remained now was a solid performance in the North Island stroke play at Titirangi, Auckland and a place in the Eisenhower team would be assured. He achieved this with a four round total of 293 to tie with a young Simon Owen for sixth equal position. Stuart Jones would take out the title on 286 and regain his place in the New Zealand team.

Ross Murray recovered from a disastrous 81 in the second round with scores of 70 and 68 to finish fifth to ensure his selection. The 23 year old from Dunedin, Geoff Clarke, finished second behind Jones on 289 and replaced John Durry in the New Zealand team who had a disappointing tournament finishing on 301.

R.M. Barltrop and B. C. Rafferty who finished third and fourth respectively were named the two reserves. T. P. McLean reported that there were no surprises in selection and that this was the best team chosen since the 1958 team that finished three strokes behind the winners after leading going into the final round.

The New Zealand golf administrators had learnt their lessons from Melbourne and ensured the team would have the necessary build up to give the team the best chance of success. They arrived ten days prior to the event starting and competed in the Spanish Amateur championship to give the team some quality competition and practice in similar conditions they would confront in Madrid.

They also assembled in Auckland in early August to play a team of professionals at the Grange club to get some much needed competition having just come out of a cold winter in the south.

McDougall headed the scoring with a 73, Jones had 75, Clarke 77 and Murray 78. John Croskery would lead the professionals with 74, followed by Frank Malloy on 76, Frank Buckler 78 and Dennis Sullivan 79. The overall result was a win to the amateurs with a combined total of 225 for the best three counting scores. The professionals had 228.

New Zealand arrived early in Spain and along with several other teams competing in the Eisenhower played in the Spanish Amateur. All four NZ players would qualify in the top 16 and advance to the match play. Jones made it all the way to the final losing to a 17 year old Spanish golfer E. de la Riva 2 and 1.

Although the Spaniards and Australians rated New Zealand as front runners to take out the Eisenhower most pundits had the United States team as the favorite followed by South Africa, Australia and Britain. The players had to endure a heat wave in the lead up to the start of the tournament where temperatures had reached 100 degrees the day before the first round. It was going to be tough going on the Real Club de la Puerta de Hierro course measuring 7,043yards and as hilly as Augusta National.

Day 1

MADRID: The NZPA staff correspondent ALAN GRAHAM would report back under the headline;

TEAM LYING FIFTH - McDougall has best NZ score

A fighting recovery by E. J. McDougall from four over par at the 12th hole to be square with par at the 18th helped NZ to fifth place of the Eisenhower Cup here today.

McDougall's round was amazingly varied as he hit four birdies and an eagle.

New Zealand's score of 220 put it seven off the hot pace of 213, three under par set by the United States.

The most notable feat of the day was a 10 on the second by Australia's top player, Kevin Donohoe, who broke his No. 9 iron on a tree while taking six to get out of some rough prairie.

Day 2

ALAN GRAHAM would write under the headline;

KIWI'S GOLF FAMILY APPLUADS 'FATHER JONES'

S. G. Jones, the top amateur golfer in New Zealand for most of the past 20 years, desperately needed to score well in the second round of the Eisenhower trophy world golf teams' event yesterday.

For, in spite of a brilliant record elsewhere, Jones had never done well in this major event and at the age of 45 he must feel this Eisenhower, his sixth, will probably be his last.

Thus when "Father" Jones turned in a round of 70, the entire New Zealand party here breathed a sigh of relief. It was plain that all the team, the national woman' team watching the play and the small family of Kiwi supporters were all urging Jones on.

In 20 previous Eisenhower rounds had not beaten 73 and one year (Rome) his best was 77, both of which are ridiculous figures for a man of his class.

Satisfying

"I hit the ball really well today. It was a most satisfying round," Jones said.

Yesterday he had four birdies in his round. And, after encountering a bad lie in a bunker at the first hole, made only one other mistake, this at the 12th where he three putted.

With Geoff Clarke scoring 71 and both McDougall and Murray 73 New Zealand had moved up to fourth equal with Canada and just one stroke behind South Africa and Mexico. The United States maintained their seven stroke lead.

Day 3

The headline after day three would be; **CLARKE HAS BEST ROUND - NZ maintains fourth position in cup golf.**

29 Putts

Clarke owed his sub-par round to his putter, for whenever his woods or irons got him into trouble, his almost unerring putter saved the day.

Clarke came to Madrid as a newcomer to Eisenhower Cup golf and shot a 75 on the first day which the team did not need to count. Since then he has two 71s and is now very much a strong man in this very good field.

Day 4.

NZPA Staff Correspondent ALAN GRAHAM, at the end of Day 4, went with **Big Ted Just Man For Pressure Putts - KIWI GOLFERS 2nd.**

After a tremendous four-nation struggle through-out the final day yesterday, the New Zealand amateur golf team snatched second place in the Eisenhower trophy world tournament. They finished 12 strokes behind the unbeatable United States side.

It was New Zealand's finest ever placing in the Eisenhower, and in the tense, final holes, New Zealand found just the man in Ted McDougall to come home in 70, two under par.

South Africa were a stroke away third, with Australia another stroke behind for fourth.

With all the pressure in the world upon him, McDougall played the second nine magnificently, scoring one birdie at the long 15th and saving a par with an eight-foot putt at the 17th when the tension was just about as thick as it can get in amateur golf.

New Zealand's other rounds were 73 by S. G. Jones, 74 by G. Clarke and 75 by R. C. Murray.

The entire New Zealand team were among the top 15 in the individual rankings and with T. Kite, of America, failing to finish because of a stomach upset, this was something New Zealand had all to its self.

The Kiwis began the last day in fourth place and by lunch time they were still in fourth place, although Mexico had replaced South Africa as one of the teams ahead of them.

Clarke, with two 71s under his belt on two previous days, had lost his fine touch around the greens and had returned a 74, needing birdies on the last two holes to salvage his day.

Then Murray came in on 75, disappointed after spoiling his first half with a drive hooked into some polo stables on the ninth, and battling throughout the second half with bunkers, missed putts and pushed irons.

Big News

Jones was still out there and his first half of 36, while not improving New Zealand's chances, did not worsen them.

Then came big news. T. Gale (Australia) had crashed with a 41 on the first half. D. Symons (South Africa) was home in a miserable 79.

T. Lehman (Mexico) was in the same polo stables as Murray on the ninth, and H. Alvarz was struggling.

Even the United States, previously unassailable in front, were in trouble, for T. Kite, the 20-year old Texan, who ignored medical advice, turned in one over par.

To play such golf was courageous, but he could not go on. Now the last American on the course, L. Wadkins, could not afford too many bad shots, or disqualification.

Then from the 12th came disastrous news of Jones. His second at the 464-yard hole had disappeared down a steep bank into some trees. His first shot there had not made the fairway and he finally took seven.

But Jones was not sunk yet. An eagle putt from 25-feet dropped into the hole to get him back two shots at the 15th, and then at the 18th putting from just off the green, Jones sank an even longer one.

All told a round of 73, just one over par, which seemed an almost unattainable score after the disastrous 12th.

Importantly, New Zealand were now narrowly in second place, equal with South Africa and Australia, with Mexico just behind. It was all on McDougall, the burly Scots-born laddie who came to New Zealand at the age of 14.

Response

And how well he responded! A bunkered drive at the first hole was his only shot dropped to par in the entire round, and as Clarke put it: "If we've got to have pressure like this, Ted's just the man we need."

A long putt gave him a birdie at the fourth; a great approach iron another at the fifth and, when he was struggling for pars at the sixth and seventh, he rammed in six-footers as if he never missed them.

By the tenth-hole McDougall knew that New Zealand now had a real chance for second place and this improved when T. Gresham (Australia) took a six on the twelfth in almost the same circumstances as Jones's seven on the same hole.

Could South Africa fight back? D. Hayes, was on the course as their last man, just behind McDougall.

Then, with McDougall on the 14th tee, came news from behind: Hayes had bogeyed two holes. New Zealand were now two shots clear of Australia, one clear of South Africa and three clear of Mexico.

Near Eagle

McDougall putted for birdie on the on the 14th. The ball slid well past the hole. Gresham putted for a birdie on the hole behind. He missed McDougall sank his 3-foot return, Hayes a par.

McDougall scored a birdie at 15, inches off an eagle. Gresham notched a fighting par at 14 after being in the trees. Hayes had a par and Mexico were now out of the running, but only just.

McDougall putting on 16 inches off a birdie. Gresham a birdie to restore the difference to two between Australia and New Zealand. Hayes a mere par.

South Africa now also two behind but the match wide open-if you discount the Americans, still way in front.

McDougall passed the green on the 17th, and his chip 8ft past the hole with a real pressure putt for the return. Hayes a birdie and now New Zealand now just one ahead of South Africa.

McDougall, Coolness itself sinks the eight-footer. The New Zealanders breathe again.

McDougall on 18, safely on in par figures, Gresham in the bunker at 17. Australia now three behind, but Hayes with a chance of a birdie on the last. A crowd of 2000 watch.

McDougall a safe par five on the 18th. Gresham a birdie but too late to save Australia's day. Hayes a birdie putt for the Springboks. It misses, and New Zealand are second best amateur golf result ever.

This was New Zealand's finest performance since finishing third in Rome in 1964. It was a complete team effort with no player scoring worse than 75 and all players making significant contributions at key moments throughout the tournament.

McDougall's four round total of 288 was the first time a New Zealand player had scored par for the four rounds in an Eisenhower and his total would not look out of place in the winning American team.

His feat would not be repeated until Philip Aickin achieved the same result in Switzerland in 1982.

The journalist Alistair Rowe summarized the New Zealand performance under the headline **-Faith Not Misplaced**. His report went as follows -
TEAM manager Peter Smyth must have been extraordinarily (and justifiably) proud of the New Zealand amateur golf side of four which came dramatically from the rear to sneak second place, ahead of South Africa and Australia-and a host of other great golfing countries as well-in the recent world championships in Madrid for the Eisenhower Trophy.

In this well-tried combination of Jones, Murray, Clarke and the mighty McDougall (massive of frame, massive of heart, imperturbable in approach when the chips were really down) New Zealand had an aggregation which must have compelled the admiration of spectators and fellow competitors in Madrid, and if ever there were a complete vindication of selectorial policy then Spain, 1970 provided it. The New Zealand Council, naturally, was delighted.

This was a team event, and, happily, every New Zealander contributed his share to the side's remarkable success, and one does not exclude manager Smyth from this. He had an unshakable faith in the team's capacity: clearly, it was not misplaced - ALISTAIR ROWE.'

Results: 1970 Eisenhower Tournament - Madrid

1. United States of America

Lanny Wadkins	70	72	72	72	286
Allen Miller, III	72	71	71	73	287
Marvin Giles, III	73	73	71	72	289
Tom Kite	71	70	74	-	
Total	**213**	**213**	**214**	**217**	**857**

2. New Zealand

Ted McDougall	72	73	73	70	288
Geoff Clarke	75	71	71	74	291
Stuart Jones	75	70	75	73	293
Ross Murray	73	73	74	75	295
Total	**220**	**214**	**218**	**217**	**869**

3. South Africa

Dale Hayes	70	71	68	74	283
John Fourie	73	75	75	74	297
Hugh Baiocchi	72	80	73	73	298
Dave Symons	72	73	76	79	300
Total	**214**	**219**	**216**	**221**	**870**

4. Australia

Tony Gresham	71	74	71	71	287
Kevin Donohoe	81	70	70	75	296
Terry Gale	76	71	71	78	296
Kevin Hartley	77	74	75	74	300
Total	**224**	**215**	**212**	**220**	**871**

The New Zealand Amateur was played soon after McDougall returned home from Spain. He would be the only team member to compete as the others had remained in Europe for a few weeks of rest and relaxation.

It would be a successful tournament. He paired up with his former team mate from 1969 Graeme Brown to win the NZ foursomes and then top qualified for the match play with rounds of 75 and 71 on the par 72 Hokowhitu course in Palmerston North.

McDougall would cruise to victory in the early rounds until he came up against the recently qualified lawyer Bruce Taylor of Christchurch in the semi-final. He gave McDougall a torrid test before Ted eventually expunged Taylor 2 and 1 from the results board.

His opponent in the final was Robin Dailey from Dannevirke who surprisingly beat the defending champion Graham Stevenson in the other semi-final.

McDougall was in complete control in the thirty six-hole final played on a very wet Hokowhitu course and ran out the winner 5 and 4. It was his second amateur title and came on the same course where he won in 1957. He again had his Pukekohe High school friend and best man David Adams as his caddy.

Ted would finish his grand year off by winning the Bledisloe Cup as the leading amateur in the NZ Open with a two under par total of 282 held on the Grange course in Auckland. Bob Charles, his team mate from 1958, broke Kel Nagle's run of three consecutive NZ Open titles by winning with a total score of 271.

The feats of McDougall in 1970 would not go unnoticed by the wider New Zealand sporting public. The media nominated McDougall as one of their six picks to take out the Murray Halberg Trust New Zealand Sportsman of the Year award.

He was nominated alongside some of New Zealand's great sports persons. The six were Harry Kent (Cycling), Bryan Williams (Rugby), Sylvia Potts (Athletics), Glenn Turner (Cricket), Dick Quax (Athletics) and Ted McDougall (Golf). The award went to Harry Kent for his achievements in the world cycling championships and his gold medal at the Commonwealth

Games in Edinburgh.

McDougall had now once and for all silenced and extinguished his many critics.

The Hendry Family at Braefoot, Monifieth. Ted's mother Jane far left. William back left. Jock back right.

Jock Hendry, Monifieth 1912

John Panton left, Johnny Murray right, outside Pitlochry Proshop circa 1947

Edward, Jane, Eddie & Margaret, Pukekohe 1952

Dan Bryant and Edward at the NZ Open, 1955

The final group of Guy Wolstenholme, William Hyndman III, and Edward McDougall, St Andrews 1958

Feel the Power, Ngamutu 1959

Exhibition match with Billy Casper, Lochiel 1969.

With Gary Player, South Africa 1975

8 BUENOS AIRES 1972

It had been a remarkable three years since recovering from his back injury in 1967. Ted's good form would continue into 1971 when he tied first with Trevor Ormsby and Peter Creighton in the Waikato Stroke play on a score of 288 however it would be Ormsby who would win the playoff in the dark at St Andrews. This was a good omen as all the Waikato players were in good form heading into the interprovincial to be played on home soil at Lochiel.

Waikato didn't disappoint their loyal supporters and they were unbeaten and leading the competition heading into the final day. There would however be a major upset in the morning when Mid-South Canterbury beat Waikato 4-1. The consequence of this loss meant in the final round Waikato had to beat Manawatu-Wanganui 5-0 and Canterbury had to lose at least one game against Mid-South Canterbury for Waikato to be crowned champions for a second time.

It would be one of the closest finishes in the history of the Freyberg as Waikato did their part by winning 5-0 and so it would come down to the final match between Ross Murray (Mid-South Canterbury) and Bruce Taylor (Canterbury) to determine the outcome of the tournament. Murray obliged when he halved the final hole against Taylor for a half to ensure the 1 game for Mid-South Canterbury, who already had half a game, and give Waikato a crucial half a point winning margin over Canterbury. The final points were Waikato 6 points (23.5 individual matches) and Canterbury 6 points (23 individual matches).

The journalist Winston Hooper summarized the performance of each Waikato player as follows;

DRAWCARD

McDougall, *no matter what the loyal supporters of Murray, Jones etc may say, still the big draw card in New Zealand amateur golf, finished the tournament with three wins, two halves and two losses. His defeats were at the hands of the two unbeaten players at the tournament R. M. Barltrop (Wellington) seven straight wins, and R. C. Murray, six wins and a half.*

Creighton, *in many minds the player of the tournament and obviously now a strong contender to regain his place in the New Zealand side, had six wins and a loss, the latter to G. K. McKinnon in the opening round.*

Ormsby, *three wins, one half, three losses, came right at the end after an indifferent start.*

Reid, *who fulfilled his big ambition in golf by being in a Freyberg winning team, had five wins and two losses and showed himself to be a much under-rated player.*

Stevenson *as valuable a number five as any side could have, also had five wins and two losses.*

And for Mr. Nelson Robinson, the team manager, it was a winning debut into the Freyberg.

It was a confident McDougall that then went to the Hutt Club in Wellington to defend his National Amateur title. Unfortunately he would have to withdraw in the very early stages of the tournament with a re-occurrence of his troublesome back. He was now constantly in significant pain and once again was admitted to Waikato Hospital where he underwent major surgery.

It was another bitter disappointment as he had to withdraw from the New Zealand team to contest the Commonwealth tournament featuring the best players from South Africa, Australia, Canada and Great Britain and Ireland and to make matters worse it was to be played on one of his favorite golf courses the Middlemore course in Auckland.

Ted took a break from top line competition for the remaining year and the early part 1972 to recover from the surgery and when he played in the Waikato Stroke Play in April he was reasonably happy with his fifth place finish albeit on a score of 305 which was well below his usual performance and expectations.

The Waikato selectors kept faith with McDougall when they selected him at number 1 to contest the Freyberg in Napier. It was the same team that had won at Lochiel except Reid would play at 5 and Ormsby at 4. It would be another very closely fought tournament and again would come down to individual games when Waikato tied with Otago on 5 and a half points each. Waikato ultimately won by virtue of an extra half an individual game more than Otago.

The hero for Waikato was Trevor Ormsby when in the penultimate round he would overcome a 4-hole deficit after ten holes to play the best nine holes of his life in beating John Durry 1up and gain a vital half point against Wellington.

As for McDougall he would finish the tournament with 5 wins, a half, and 1 loss to show the selectors he was ready and able to re-enter the New Zealand side. Towards the end of his match in the final round against Peter Burney of Auckland he went eagle, birdie, and birdie for a 4 and 2 win.

The selection of the New Zealand team for the Eisenhower to be played in Buenos Aires was relatively straight forward. Since finishing second in Spain all four players of that team had continued with their good form with only Rodney Barltrop from Wellington being a serious contender to displace any of the incumbents'.

Clarke had been the leading amateur at 1971 NZ Open and won the 1972 South Island stroke play. Murray had won the 1971 South Island stroke play and Jones had won the 1971 Amateur and the 1972 North Island stroke play.

Although plagued with injury during this period McDougall had shown enough good form in leading Waikato to victories in both the 1971 and 1972 Freyberg Rose Bowl tournaments. Hence it was the same team that had performed so well in Spain in 1970 that would head to Buenos Aires.

The USA team prevailed with Ben Crenshaw (68) and Marvin Giles III (71) leading the way in the morning of the final day. Australia had gone into the final round with a three stroke lead over the Americans but couldn't match their hot pace set in the morning to finish five behind comfortably in second place.

Tony Gresham was the stand out player for Australia finishing first individual on 285 with Crenshaw and Giles III a further two behind. The New Zealand team finished fifth equal with the hosts Argentina just six strokes behind third place South Africa.

Ross Murray and Stuart Jones had New Zealand in a handy position after two rounds after they both shot 71s in the second round.

Clarke had a solid 74 in the third round but was just off his usual high standard in the other rounds. McDougall finished strongly with two 72s but they couldn't quite combine well enough as a team to get that low three round total they needed to finish in the top three.

Ross Murray and Stuart Jones tied 9th equal with Michael Bonallack and Charles Green from Great Britain and Ireland in the individual standings on 295.

This was Stuart Jones's first top ten individual performance in an Eisenhower and it would also be his last of seven appearances.

1. United States of America

Ben Crenshaw	74	76	69	68	287
Marvin Giles, III	73	73	70	71	287
Mark Heyes	74	71	71	75	291
Martin West, III	76	76	76	79	307
Total	**221**	**220**	**210**	**214**	**865**

2. Australia

Tony Gresham	70	69	73	73	285
Terry Gale	71	80	68	77	296
Noel Ratcliffe	75	75	73	73	296
Michael Cahill	74	75	75	76	300
Total	**215**	**219**	**214**	**222**	**870**

3. South Africa

Neville Sandelson	75	72	72	69	288
Coen Dreyer	77	72	70	75	294
Johann Murray	72	74	72	78	296
Kevin Suddards ·	79	79	74	79	311
Total	**224**	**218**	**214**	**222**	**878**

5. New Zealand

Ross Murray	73	71	75	76	295
Stuart Jones	74	71	76	74	295
Ted McDougall	76	78	72	72	298
Geoff Clarke	77	76	74	77	304
Total	**223**	**218**	**221**	**222**	**884**

9 THE TEETH OF THE DOG 1974

Pete Dye's 'Teeth of the Dog' built in 1971 is ranked as the No. 1 course in the Caribbean and 43rd in the top 100 courses, worldwide.

"The opportunity to carve out Teeth of the Dog was once-in-a-lifetime experience", Pete Dye wrote in his book, Burry me in a Pot Bunker. Without proper heavy machinery to crack the coral, the tireless Dominican crew used sledgehammers, pickaxes and chisels. The result was a true masterpiece!

Tricky shots such as a devilish dogleg and signature Dye obstacles captivate the world's best. Toss-in trade winds courtesy of Mather Nature and "seven holes created by god", said Dye who lays claim to creating only the other eleven and you discover the magnetic force of this amazing course.

But beware if you dare to challenge the Dog "at some point in your game, this DOG WILL bite you - guaranteed ", chuckles Gillis Gagnon, Director of Golf at Casa de Campo.

This course would be the venue for the 1974 Eisenhower Trophy.

On returning home to New Zealand McDougall did not feel comfortable with his back and made the decision to have a complete rest from competitive golf for an extended period of time. He therefore did not play the 1972 NZ Amateur played at Waitikiri which was won, for the first time, by his team mate and now good friend Ross Murray.

He did not play in the Waikato trials in the early part of 1973 and was

117

unavailable for selection for Waikato to contest the Freyberg Rose Bowl which was won by Geoff Clarke's Otago team at Russley. He would also skip the North Island at Titirangi won by Ken Hankin of Auckland.

When the NZ Amateur came around in November to be played at Springfield in Rotorua Ted now felt he was ready to play top flight golf again. It had been close to twelve months since the Eisenhower and it was rumored McDougall's golf had effectively come to an end.

Over the years, chronic troubles with his spine had accumulated to the stage where he had been told, pretty straight, that he would never again be capable of top golf.

In 1971 "Big Ted" had bit the bullet - he elected an operation which fused two of the disks in his spine. He had come back too soon after that operation however- after this latest twelve month break he was feeling fit and ready to go again.

He teamed up with Ross Murray in the foursomes where they finished well down the field with rounds of 73 and 78.

They both fared much better in the two qualifying rounds. McDougall shot 71 and 70 and Murray 70 and 72 to qualify third and fourth respectively.

Top qualifier was a new emerging talent in the form Tauranga's Mike Nicholson who fired a second round five under 66 after a first round 72. In second place was Ken Hankin with rounds of 69 and 70. Hankin was on a nice run of good form since winning the North Island earlier in the year.

There were only 32 qualifiers this year rather than 64 that had been in the past. Stuart Jones was fortunate to make the cut on 151 when he beat A. C. Relph in a playoff for the 32nd spot.

McDougall beat his Waikato team mate Stuart Reid in the first round 2 and 1 and Sloan Morpeth 3 and 2 in the second round before overcoming Rodney Barltrop 1 up in the quarter final played in torrential rain.

Barltrop had earlier beaten his fellow Wellington team mate Richard Coombes 6 and 5 in the first round.

Ross Murray had bowed out in the first round and it was Stuart Jones who would emerge from bottom qualifier to make the semi-final to be played against another youthful talent Owen Kendall. The top qualifier Mike Nicholson had maintained his hot form and cruised through all his rounds to reach the semi-final to face McDougall.

This time around it would be youth that would prevail over experience with Nicholson in blistering form to be seven under par when he beat McDougall 5 and 4 and Kendall edged Jones 1up.

In the final Kendall was no match for the in-form Nicholson going down 7 and 6.

The Waikato selectors kept faith with McDougall when they named him No. 1 for the Freyberg Rose Bowl to be played at Mt Denby, Whangarei in May 1974. There were some young new faces in the Waikato team with only McDougall and Ormsby remaining from the 1971 and 1972 winning teams. The new young talent introduced to the team were Stuart Reese, Colin Taylor and Sloan Morpeth.

Waikato only lost to Wellington, in the third round, on their way to recording six other victories for six points to again win the Freyberg with Hawkes Bay finishing second.

Ted had five wins out seven matches with notable wins over Nicholson, Hankin and Murray. Waikato had now won the Freyberg in three of the last four years and four of the last seven years since their maiden victory in 1968.

The selection for the New Zealand team to contest the Eisenhower would essentially be determined by performances in the North and South Island stroke play events played over the same weekend.

The South Island had at this time some very strong players however it would be Murray on a score of 287 and Clarke two shots further back on 289 that would head off the challenges from Paul Hartstone, Jim Lapsley and Geoff Saunders on the Waitikiri course.

Up north at the Hutt in Wellington Mike Nicholson ran out the winner on 281 including a pair of four under 66s. It was very close for second with Reese just edging Kendall by a shot and McDougall a couple more back on

286.

Richard Coombes looked the player to beat after a first round 65 however he capitulated in the third round with a nine over 79 and finished tied 5th with Rod Barltrop on 288.

There were a least five or six players that had a realistic chance of selection and the selectors were clearly undecided and hence at short notice arranged a 'North v South' trial at Heretaunga.

Only twelve players were invited with players of the caliber of Rodney Barltrop and Ken Hankin not invited. It was all very strange indeed.

At the completion of the North Island and South Island stroke play championships it appeared the team should be Murray and Clarke from down south to join Nicholson and McDougall from up north.

The two unlucky players being Owen Kendall and Stuart Reese who on balance hadn't quite done enough to replace any of the more experienced members of the team.

The three rounds of trial golf provided a surprise winner in the form of Richard Coombes. McDougall was second equal with Jim Lapsley and Ross Murray was a further stroke back in fourth.

Kendall and Clarke were well off the pace as was Reese. The selectors, to the surprise of most pundits, selected Coombes along with Nicholson, McDougall and Murray.

Geoff Clarke was now the unlucky one to miss selection.

There was also to be another break from tradition with the New Zealand Amateur again brought forward and the NZ team using the event as a warm up for the Eisenhower.

The Amateur, played on the tight tree lined Manukau course in Auckland and nothing close to what they would experience at the Eisenhower, would not be the dress rehearsal the selectors were hoping for.

McDougall showed he was still in good form with rounds of 72 and 68 to qualify in second spot two shots behind the NZ team reserve Owen

Kendall who fired 71 and then set a new course record with a second round four under par 67.

Nicholson had a couple of solid 72s however Murray just made the cut by one shot on 150 and Coombes missed qualifying for the match play altogether on 153.

In the match play Murray and Nicholson were knocked out early however McDougall had a couple of nice wins when he defeated Graeme Stevenson in the first round and Stuart Jones in the second round, however he couldn't maintain his winning streak and lost to Ken Hankin in the quarter final.

There was some irony when Rodney Barltrop defeated Ken Hankin 3 and 1 in the final. These were two players who had been in relatively good form over the past two years but the selectors deemed not good enough to be included in their NZ trial at Herataunga!

Immediately following the NZ Amateur the NZ team were on a flight to face the Cajuiles 'Teeth of the Dog'

The 1974 Eisenhower was originally scheduled to be played in Kuala Lumpur however at the eleventh hour the Malaysian Government refused to admit South Africa. The event was likely to be cancelled but for the world renowned course architect Pete Dye who offered up his newly completed project in the Dominican Republic.

The New Zealand team arrived just as the woman were completing their Espirito Santo tournament. In twelve rounds of golf the NZ woman's team had only broken 80 once to finish 14th overall. Pete Dye predicted only a handful of players would break 300 in the men's event.

This was a golf course like no other that the NZ players had experienced before. As the NZ journalist Garry Ahearn, who was accompanying the team, would write -*Cajuiles was a course that had to be well thought out, and secondly, equally well played. The dominating factor was going to be the wind, an element that was very much part of the course. And the importance of yardage couldn't be over-emphasized. The course generally demanded near perfect golf.*

Typical of how the New Zealand players would fair can be exampled by McDougall's second round 78 described by Garry Ahern as follows. The best second round effort came from Ted McDougall who returned a 6 over par 78. He started with a birdie on the first but was back to square after the second. His first twelve holes in fact consisted of four pars, four birdies and four bogeys and he was still square after 13. The turning point for McDougall came at the par five 14th *when no one could believe his birdie putt from about seven feet broke sharply only an inch or two from the hole. He three putted the 15*[th]*, then after a superb tee shot at the par three 16*[th]*, he found himself with an impossible lie in the bunker. McDougall did well to drop only two shots at the 16*[th] *but he dropped another at the 17*[th] *and two at the eighteenth - 6 shots in only four holes.*

Ahearn then commented that *-this was typical of many at the tournament with the young Canadian Doug Roxburgh finishing 7, 8, and 9 for an 84 in the first round. He dropped all his 12 shots in the last three holes.*

It was therefore no surprise that the United States of America were the best equipped team to handle this course and who would again dominate. The usual suspects in the form of Great Britain & Ireland, Australia, Canada and South Africa would also struggle and it would be Japan and Brazil that would this time take out the minor medals.

The New Zealand team finished a disappointing 15th, their worst performance to date. The team was forever looking for explanations. Ahearn would write *-without making excuses the breaks just didn't go the way of the New Zealanders. - Almost invariable they were close to par rounds, but just couldn't sustain it over the final few holes.*

In reviewing the golf year in the 1975 DB Golf Annual the great NZ journalist T. P. McLean would quote Sir Bob Charles and Ross Murray who both came out firing after New Zealand's poor performance at the Eisenhower. They said words to the effect that New Zealand Golf had not kept up with international developments and that the general standard of New Zealand golf courses were well below that of international standard and the standard of amateur golf was "*terrible - in fact, quite pathetic*".

These were extreme comments indeed.

In 1973 there were no international representative events at all for the New Zealand players. There were a number of talented players emerging on the scene with the likes of Nicholson, Kendall, Barltrop, Alldred, Coombes and

Reese to challenge Jones, Murray, McDougall and Clarke.

They were all scoring some very low scores in national events but if these young talented players are not given some international exposure and experience it makes it very difficult for them to break through to that next level.

Yes New Zealand is limited by the small number of golf course that approach anywhere near the standard of the top international courses.

Perhaps where New Zealand lets itself down is in course maintenance. The standard of green keeping, even today, is well below that of international standard and it is not always necessarily a question of finances but more about education and priorities for the board members and committees that manage their courses.

Pete Dye would indeed be proved correct when only four players of the best amateurs in the world would break 300!

Results: 1974 Eisenhower, Dominican Republic

1. United States

Jerome Pate	73	77	73	71	294
George Burns, III	74	76	70	77	297
Gary Koch	79	70	76	76	301
Curtis Strange	77	75	77	77	306
Total	**224**	**221**	**219**	**224**	**888**

2. Japan

Satoshi Yamazaki	73	75	76	71	295
Tsutomu Irie	75	77	73	80	305
Ginjiro Nakabe	83	80	70	76	309
Tetsuo Sakata	78	74	77	81	310
Total	**226**	**226**	**219**	**227**	**898**

3. Brazil

Jayme Gonzalez	73	74	74	73	294
Jose Diniz	73	80	70	77	300
Ricardo Rossi	79	75	77	79	310
Rafael Navarro	79	80	86	76	321
Total	**225**	**229**	**221**	**226**	**901**

5 Australia

Terry Gale	78	75	75	72	300
Tony Gresham	78	78	77	75	308
Phil Wood	79	81	77	74	311
Colin Kaye	83	78	77	79	317
Total	**235**	**231**	**229**	**221**	**916**

15. New Zealand

Ted McDougall	81	78	78	79	316
Richard Coombes	80	81	78	78	317
Ross Murray	82	79	80	78	319
Mike Nicholson	80	80	86	77	323
Total	**241**	**237**	**236**	**233**	**947**

10 SOUTH AFRICA 1975

Young 21 year old Stuart Reese was the new threat to McDougall's supremacy in the Waikato when he retained the Waikato stroke play title at Hamilton and was named ahead of McDougall to contest the Freyberg at Belmont in Wanganui.

There was more than the usual amount of focus on the performances of individuals as the New Zealand selectors were in attendance with the naming of, later in the year, the New Zealand team to contest the Commonwealth tournament to be played in South Africa.

A new look Auckland team which included Peter Burney, Stephen Partridge, Pat Garner, Rod White and Ken Hankin emerged victorious ahead of the more fancied teams of Wellington, Hawkes Bay and the defending champions Waikato.

Auckland, who had finished near the tail of the field the year before, came from behind in the early stages of their final match against the local Manawatu-Wanganui team to win 3-2 and take out the Freyberg Rose Bowl.

The player of the tournament was Stuart Jones. The Hawkes Bay number one recorded seven wins from seven matches which included wins over; Osman, Nicholson, Bonnington, Murray, McCormack, Clarke and Hartstone.

The New Zealand selectors had already indicated the six man team would be a mix of experience and youth with the general consensus that Jones along with McDougall, who had five wins, would be the two experienced players that would be the foundation of the team.

There was an abundance of talent on display from which selectors could call upon however they would have been disappointed by the form shown in the Freyberg of the three most likely youthful contenders Chris Alldred, Mike Nicholson and Owen Kendall.

The North Island and South Island championships would now play a pivotal role in who was selected for New Zealand. Unfortunately both events wouldn't have the desired results. The North Island was plagued by atrocious weather conditions and the event reduced to three rounds and absurdly the South Island was now a match play event!

In 1969 the North Island championship was altered to a match play event and was a complete disaster and now the people in the halls of power were about to make the same mistake again.

The North Island and South Island events are the only national amateur stroke play events in the country. These are the two events that are a true indicator of a players form and generally attract the best fields. Why the national administrators would want to 'tinker' with this format is beyond comprehension.

The North Island was played on the new par 73 Stewart Alexander course measuring over 7000 yards. On a very wet course, and the first round abandoned. Rodney Barltrop and Chris Alldred tied first on a score of 223 followed by Rex Godso (224) Mike Nicholson (225) and Stuart Reese and Owen Kendall on (226).

McDougall, who was trying out a new set of McGregor clubs, was in contention after two rounds with rounds of 79 and 74 however in the final round, after hitting a ball out of bounds, numerous three putts and a dreaded shank, finished with a disastrous 81 which saw him slip down the field to finish in 19th position. It was his worst result in a national event since the North Island at Levin in 1962.

Meanwhile down south Paul Hartstone won the South Island at Levels in Timaru beating Robbie Bell of Ashburton 5 and 3 in the final. Hartstone then dropped a bombshell when he announced he was unavailable for the R and A (Commonwealth) Tournament in South Africa in November.

But it wasn't his declared opposition to South Africa's sporting policies that resulted in his decision. Education and his future were of first concern, Hartstone making it quite clear that his career was No.1 in his book.

Immediately after the North Island and South Island events the selectors kept faith with McDougall and along with Rodney Barltrop represented New Zealand at an international event in Bogota Colombia, South America.

Ted McDougall and Rodney Barltrop played soundly in the rarefied atmosphere some 8000ft above sea level and finished equal sixth with both players scoring 298.

McDougall and Barltrop arrived back in New Zealand just in time to compete in the inaugural Peter Stuyvesant sponsored North Island versus South Island tournament to be played at Russley in Christchurch.

The format would consist of the best 24 players from each Island and the best six junior players from each Island.

It was August, which is still winter in New Zealand, and there had been a major storm earlier in the month with a number of trees severely damaged. The event was in doubt however the weather improved later in the week and most of the debris cleared from the course.

Saturday dawned a still day with clear blue skies albeit on the chilly side.

There were to be two rounds played on the Saturday with the final round on Sunday. Having just come off the high veldt in South America McDougall would produce perhaps the finest golf of his entire career with rounds of 66 and 67 on the par 73 course to be 13 under par and eight shots clear of his nearest rival Alex Bonnington.

Stuart Jones, on a score of 150, would enquire -"*is McDougall playing the same course as the rest of us?!*"

McDougall cooled down with a 76 in the final round played in cold wet conditions but still won by six shots from Alex Bonnington.

Below - McDougall's score card for the first 36 holes of the Peter

Stuyvesant played at Russley, 1975.

HOLE	1	2	3	4	5	6	7	8	9	OUT	10	11	12	13	14	15	16	17	18	IN	OUT	TOTAL
METRES	298	432	130	367	385	459	189	373	454	3087	181	311	356	426	398	186	500	355	372	3085	3087	6172
YARDS	326	472	142	401	421	502	207	408	496	3376	198	340	389	466	435	203	547	388	407	3374	3376	6750
PAR	4	5	3	4	4	5	3	4	5	37	3	4	4	5	4	3	5	4	4	36	37	73
ROUND 1	3	4	3	4	4	4	2	4	5	33	3	4	4	4	4	3	4	3	4	33	33	66
ROUND 2	4	4	2	4	4	5	3	5	4	35	3	4	3	4	3	2	5	5	3	32	35	67

Following the Peter Stuyvesant the New Zealand team was named to compete in the Commonwealth tournament in Durban, South Africa.

Included were McDougall, Clarke, Nicholson, Reese, Rod Barltrop and Jones who was returning after being unavailable for the Dominican Republic.

Ross Murray missed selection for the first time since 1961. He made his debut for New Zealand in 1959 at the Commonwealth tournament also played in South Africa. He didn't make the team for the Eisenhower in 1960 but played in every NZ team from 1961 until 1974.

The Commonwealth tournament was played amongst only four nations being Great Britain, Canada, New Zealand and the hosts South Africa. Australia withdrew for political reasons.

It was unfortunate for the Australian players who would miss out on playing with some of the future stars of world golf in the form of Nick Faldo and Sandy Lyle.

The New Zealand team left Auckland airport, without a protestor in sight, bound for Johannesburg via London where they stopped over for a round of golf at Wentworth.

On arrival in J'burg the team was meet by Bob Charles who was hosting the teams along with Gary Player. The team stayed and practiced in J'burg for a few days and also joined Gary Player in celebrating his 40th birthday.

It was then onto Capetown and the Mowbray course where the New Zealand team would compete against the other Commonwealth teams in a 72 hole stroke event.

McDougall with rounds of 77, 71, and 73 led Ian Hutcheon by a shot and a quality field that included Nick Faldo, Sandy Lyle and Michael Bonallack.

Ted stumbled to a final round 79 after he lost a ball up a tree late in the round in the windy conditions.

He finished fourth alongside Hutcheon on 300 two shots behind Faldo who shot a brilliant 72 in the conditions and won in a playoff against Stuart Jones and Gerard Williams.

Royal Durban was the venue for match play event. The tournament was an outstanding teams' event from the first tee shot until the final putt, the one disappointing aspect being the absence of the Australian team due to political pressures prohibiting sporting contacts with South Africa.

New Zealand gave the very talented Great Britain team a fright in their first match. McDougall and Reese were the only New Zealand pair to win their foursomes match in the morning by defeating Dave Greig and George McGregor 4 and 3.

New Zealand trailed Britain 2-1 at the completion of the foursomes.

Reese and McDougall maintained their good morning form with wins over Geoff Marks and David Greig in the afternoon singles matches.

Clarke and Barltrop both halved their matches against Hutcheon and McGregor however with Jones losing to Sandy Lyle 3 and 2 it came down to the Faldo/Nicholson match to determine the outcome which Faldo won on the last hole for a 1up win.

The singles matches were therefore shared 3 a piece and Britain won narrowly 5-4.

South Africa defeated Canada 6 ½-2 ½ in the other match.

New Zealand was in the same situation again the following day when they trailed South Africa 2-1 after the morning foursomes with Jones and Clarke the winning combination this time.

McDougall led the way again in the singles with another convincing win 4 and 3 over Peter Todt. Clarke and Jones repeated their good morning form with wins over Suddards and Heyneman.

Stuart Reese and Rodney Barltrop had losses to Stewart and Levenson however when Mike Nicholson held on to defeat Coen Dryer on the last green New Zealand had won the singles 4-2 for an unlikely 5-4 victory.

The inexperienced Canadian team caused a boil over when they comprehensively beat the British team 6-3.

This meant all four teams had recorded one win each heading into the final matches. It was a dream situation for spectators and tournament organizers.

The New Zealanders were comprehensively beaten by the Canadians 3-0 in the morning foursomes and could only manage a win from Nicholson and a half from Clarke in the afternoon singles to be soundly beaten 7 ½-1 ½.

Yes, a disappointing but by no means disastrous end for New Zealand to a fine tournament.

Great Britain won their match narrowly against South Africa hence it was the unfancied Canadian team comprising Doug Roxburgh, Robbie Jackson, Jim Nelford, Ces Fergusson, Ken Tamble and Dave Webber who were the champions on superior individual games.

The New Zealand Amateur had been played just prior to leaving for South Africa and leading into the tournament McDougall and Reese were the clear favorites to take out the title.

The New Zealand Press Association would report on the qualifying rounds as follows;

The 20-year old North Auckland green keeper, Rick Barker, consolidated his overnight lead in the national amateur golf championship at Nelson yesterday and finished the highest qualifier with a 36-hole total of 139.

His steady play produced a par 71 and won him the St Andrew's Salver with a qualifying score that was one shot clear of the New Zealand representatives Stuart Reese of Hamilton, and Ted McDougall, of Tokoroa.

Barker, Reese and McDougall were well clear of the field, the closest qualifiers taking two-over-par totals of 144. They are John Durry, of Paraparaumu, Peter Burney of

Manukau, Ian Donaldson of Greymouth, and Denis Beggs, of Rangiora, who turned in the best round of the day, a two-under-par 69.

The 1973 champion, and present national representative, Mike Nicholson, of Tauranga, followed his disappointing first-round 79 with a poor six-over 77. He did not qualify. Nor did the New Zealand reserve, Alex Bonnington, who scored 78, to add to his disastrous first-round 83.

The tensest part of the day was the play-off by 11 golfers for the six remaining qualifying spots. Twenty-six players shot 150 or better, leaving the 11 on 151 to play-off. Four qualified on the very tense first hole, Graeme McLean, of Blenheim, sinking a 10-foot birdie putt, and Rex Godso, of Pukekohe, Stephen Street, of Harewood, and Daryl Templeman, of Miramar securing pars.

Two players were eliminated: George Allan, of Westport, who picked up after hitting out of bounds, and Graham Reid, of Paraparaumu, who had a double bogey. The five remaining players who had one-overs went to the second play-off hole.

Two of them, Stephen Barron, of Paraparaumu, and Ted Webber of the Grange, clutched regulation pars to make the other two qualifiers for match-play today. The three eliminated on the second extra hole were John Fellowes, of Nelson, who hooked his second and made five, Rod Martin of Remuera, who three-putted for a five; and Murray Brown, of Waitikiri, who missed a two-footer on the first extra hole to qualify, again missing from eight feet for a five.

Of the leading players both Reese and McDougall looked to be in awesome form, and real threats to Barker's position at the head of the field. McDougall was two-under after nine holes, and he picked up another shot when he rammed home a 12-foot birdie putt on the tenth. However, he could not improve, dropping a shot on the fourteenth for a two-under 69.

Reese stormed to three-under after 11, aided by two 30-foot gulping putts for birdies on the ninth and eleventh. But he faltered with approach shots on the fourteenth and fifteenth for his second one-under-par 70.

The early rounds went according to the script for McDougall who had wins over Sloan Morpeth (Manawatu), Barry Hall (Remuera) and John Durry (Paraparaumu). Reese also had comfortable wins over G. Daines (Rarangi), Ted Webber (Grange) and J. Dixon (Harewood).

Steve Transom, the green keeper from Maraenui, ousted Rick Barker in the first round and followed this up with wins over T. Scott (Takapau) and I Cull (New Plymouth) to set up a match against Stuart Reese in one semi-final.

Ross Murray lost to Peter Burney in the first round however he in turn lost to the 15-year Stephen Barron on the 19th in the second round. The defending champion Rodney Barltrop fell to A. Smith from Carterton in the second round. Barron then defeated Smith 2 and 1 in the quarter final to set up a semi-final match against McDougall.

The New Zealand Press Association would then write -*David, in the form of the diminutive 15-year-old Stephen Barron, brought down Goliath-big Ted McDougall-in an epic semi-final of the national amateur golf championship yesterday.*

Barron, the bottom qualifier, ended the hopes of McDougall, a New Zealand representative from Tokoroa, with a rolling 20-foot birdie putt on the third extra hole.

He plays in the 36-hole final today against Stuart Reese of Hamilton.

The golden putting touch of McDougall eluded him throughout the round. He missed five short putts under 10-feet and watched in agony as 30-footers on the nineteenth and twentieth dived into the hole, but spun out.

In the other semi-final, Reese after a superb start, suffered some muddling shots before disposing of Steve Transom of Maraenui, 4 and 3.

But all the attention focused on the pint-sized Paraparaumu golfer as he defied all golfing logic. Barron, who does not have a smooth swing but does possess a never-say-die attitude, started strongly with a birdie at the sixth and a par on the eighth when McDougall was one-over to go two up.

McDougall won the tenth with a par, but lost the eleventh to a 20-foot Barron birdie, before taking the twelfth with a par to stay one down. He looked to be taking control over the confident Barron when he pared the fourteenth for the win and took the lead for the first time with another par on 16.

But the incredible Barron chipped "dead" on the seventeenth for a half, to go onto the eighteenth. After a regulation par by Barron, McDougall was left with a three foot putt for a par and a place in the final.

Somehow the ball stayed on the edge and the game went to a sudden-death play-off. McDougall's 30-foot birdie putt on 19 took a cruel turn at the last moment while Barron managed his par.

Barron holed a three-footer on the 20th for a par, while McDougall's superb birdie putt twisted out of the cup. But Barron came storming back with his 20-foot birdie on the par-3 twenty-first and, almost unbelievably, he was through to the final.

The final would prove to be an anti-climax with Reese winning the 36-hole final by a record margin 10 and 9.

11 PENINA 1976

McDougall began the 1976 season in style by winning the Waikato Stroke play for a fourth time and in the process he regained the No. 1 spot back from Reese for Freyberg Rose Bowl to be played at Timaru.

Waikato had a very strong team on paper but would have a very disappointing tournament finishing mid-table.

McDougall, after a slow start, finished with four wins and three losses for a satisfactory individual performance.

The unheralded Canterbury team of Bruce Taylor, Geoff Saunders, Dennis Beggs, Simon Robinson and C. J. Hoole went through the tournament with seven straight wins and a very convincing win leaving second place Otago in its wake.

The 1976 North Island stroke play championship played on Ted's home course would be redemption for the events that unfolded ten years earlier on the same course at the 1966 NZ Forest Products sponsored professional tournament won by Tony Jacklin and Bob Charles who tied on a score of 272. McDougall had limped round in a score of 295 with severe back pain and soon after he was hospitalized.

The North Island would be a different story altogether. The NZ Herald correspondent would report - *His score of 70, 66, 69, 73-278 on the par-72 course headed off the 22-year-old Northlander, A. W. Bonnington, by five strokes with the defending joint titleholder R. M. Barltrop (Miramar), four strokes further back in third place.*

McDougall was two under par in the bleak showery conditions of Saturday morning. He equaled his own course record in the afternoon with an impeccable 66 (34-32). This round comprised six birdies and twelve pars.

From the moment he holed a 30-foot uphill putt for an eagle three on the last green for a 69 yesterday morning his third North Island tournament title looked to be in his grasp.'

In the final round at 12.25 the clouds rolled over and almost blizzard conditions existed for much of the afternoon. McDougall played a very conservative game in the conditions hitting 18 greens and having 37 putts for a final round 73 and a comfortable victory.

Results: North Island Stroke Play - June 1976 - Tokoroa Golf Club

1	**E. J. McDougall (Tokoroa)**	**70**	**66**	**69**	**73**	**278**
2	A. W. Bonnington (Wellsford)	71	68	72	72	283
3	R. M. Barltrop (Miramar)	75	69	71	72	287
4=	P. Burney (Manukau)	74	71	73	70	288
4=	N. Gaskin (Belmont)	73	72	69	74	288
4=	P. A. Reid (Murwai)	73	69	71	75	288
7=	P. A. Maude (Hastings)	74	74	73	70	291
7=	K. R. Hankin (Titirangi)	74	73	71	73	291
9	S. F. Reese (Hamilton)	75	70	72	75	292
10=	C. E. Taylor (Hamilton)	76	74	71	72	293
10=	S. Partridge (Manukau)	74	73	74	72	293
10=	W. Simpson (Mt Maunganui)	76	69	75	73	293
10=	P. K. Creighton (Napier)	68	77	74	74	293
14	M. Barltrop (Fielding)	78	72	70	74	294
15	P. Hartstone (Napier)	79	73	68	75	295

The final trial event before the naming of the four man New Zealand team to compete at the Eisenhower to be played at Penina, Portugal was the Peter Stuyvesant.

Brian Doherty writes a succinct summary of proceedings under the headline -**Clarke now just loves hanging on.**

Geoff Clarke (St Clair) believes the best part of his golf game is that he has learnt how to hang on. And he showed that ability during the weekend to take the Peter Stuyvesant Cup tournament at Titirangi by a shot from Ted McDougall and Phil Reid.

After the first round Clarke looked to be in a hopeless position. He shot a 76, and was lucky to score that to trail Peter Maude (Hastings) by eight shots and McDougall by seven. "I'm a pretty determined fellow by nature and I needed to be, giving Ted that much start," Clarke said yesterday.

A five-under 67 on Saturday afternoon moved him to equal third, one under and one behind McDougall and two behind Maude. The final round yesterday, played for the most part in rain, became a match race between McDougall, Clarke and Muriwai's Reid, who only got into the tournament after Terry Pulman with-drew.

A three-way play-off was on as the trio all reached three under for the tournament. Maude, who found four footers beyond him, fell away in the middle stages although he rattled home with birdies on the last three holes.

Reid birdied the 13th by holing a 10-metre putt and played par golf until the last, which he bogeyed. Behind him, McDougall nearly holed an eagle chip on the 12th and birdied, as did Clarke. The 13th was expensive for McDougall, who snapped a fairway wood into deep trouble and bogeyed.

But he chipped in on the short 14th while Clarke holed a character-building putt for par. Clarke won the tournament on the 17th when he birdied from five metres. McDougall also had a chance at birdie but was forced by casual water to shift from a straightforward uphill putt to a downhiller with borrow. He Missed.

Few of the field dared to attack the pins at Titirangi. As McDougall said "The penalties over the back of the greens are so severe, it's hard to get yourself to hit it up. For Clarke the victory was a welcome return to the golden touch which saw him shoot rounds of 64, 61, 65, 68 and 69 in tournaments in Dunedin.

He injured his back three weeks ago and some of the magic was lost. He hopes that the touch will stay with the Sloan Morpeth Trophy match against Australia at Muriwai on Wednesday and the Eisenhower in Portugal coming up.

The selection of the New Zealand team was not straight forward for the selectors. McDougall and Clarke were both in grand form and were clearly the two best players in the country at this time however the make-up of the other two members was problematic.

The selectors would settle on Alex Bonnington who was the next best performed player including finishing second in the North Island stroke play and Peter Burney who was the best Auckland player having won the Auckland stroke play on four occasions however his form at the Peter Stuyvesant must have had the selectors a little worried when he finished well down the field.

The unlucky players to miss selection were Ross Murray who had returned to form after being dropped for South Africa and Rodney Barltrop who was still playing consistent golf and had represented New Zealand in Columbia and South Africa. Both these players had proven international-experience which would be in desperate need at the tough Penina layout.

The Sloan Morpeth Trophy played for between Australia and New Zealand was back on the calendar. The last time this tournament had been played was back in 1969 in Adelaide. The Australians would play NZ at the Muriwai links course just 40 minutes north of Auckland on the west coast. The teams would then travel together to Portugal with a stop-over in Los Angeles.

The Australian team was Tony Gresham, Chris Bonython, Phil Wood and Colin Kaye. The correspondent Brian Doherty would lead with **-Never-quit Clarke does trick**' '*Geoff Clarke was the right man for the job as New Zealand fought to lift the Sloan Morpeth Trophy from Australia at the Muriwai Golf Club yesterday.*

Clarke is the classic example of a winner never quitting and through his 10-year international career he has recovered from some hopeless positions to grab glory. Yesterday was another chapter of success.

The trophy looked certain to end a tie when Clarke and Colin Kaye came to the 18th green. The morning foursomes had been shared after Ted McDougall and Clarke had beaten Chris Bonython and Kaye 4 and 3 and Peter Burney and Alex Bonnington had lost 4 and 2 to Tony Gresham and Phil Wood.

In the singles, McDougall beat Bonython 5 and 4, Bonnington beat Wood 2 and 1 and Burney lost to Gresham 4 and 2. Kaye was 1 up on Clarke playing the last and was nearest to the pin.

Clarke surveyed his 25-foot breaking putt from every angle and then rammed it into the hole. Kaye, surprisingly, putted up short and Clarke had squared the match to give New Zealand the trophy 3 ½-2 ½.

Clarke cut back the-borrow to a bare minimum. "I didn't want the ball to stop above the cup," he said afterwards. Gresham the most experienced Australian, said: "Clarkie, I know you're a great putter, but that's ridiculous."

It was a grand performance by the New Zealanders, who leave this evening with the Australians for the Eisenhower Trophy tournament in Portugal. All that was missing yesterday was the Sloan Morpeth Trophy. It was thought it must still be in the Grange club, where Australia won it in 1969.

McDougall's win over Bonython was comfortable enough. He was two up after the 4th, which he eagled from 27ft, and was soon 5up.

Burney was uncharacteristically inaccurate against Gresham, missing 10 greens to the Australian's 2. Bonnington was a success. He turned three up, sinking a birdie putt on the 9th green from the same spot as in the morning. But he 4 putted the 12th and was soon back to 1 up. Wood threw a couple of great shots at Bonnington, who hung on to chip dead to the pin on the 17th to win the match.

Nothing is ever straight forward about Clarkes's game. He sank a huge putt on the 8th for a birdie and the three-putted the 9th for bogey. He turned 1 down, was square after the 14th and three-putted the 15th to be behind again. But that just set up that fighting finish.'

On the way to Portugal the New Zealand team won a three-way match with the Australian team and a local team from the Los Angeles Country Club. The New Zealand team scored 219 against 223 for the Australians and 228 for the Los Angeles Country Club. The New Zealander E. J. McDougall was the best scorer in the 18-hole event with a one-under par 70.

The Henry Cotton designed Championship Course at Penina is regarded by many as the finest course in the Algarve and beyond. The par 73 course is flanked by streams, water hazards and precarious ditches, and the course boasts an array of subtle slopes and raised greens.

To understand the difficulty of the course we can analyze the results of the Portuguese Open which was played at Penina as part of the European tour in 1975 and again in 1977 being a year either side of the Eisenhower.

In 1975 the winning score was 292 won by Hal Underwood of the United States and in 1977 only two players broke 290 won by Manuel Ramos of Spain on 287. Simon Owen from New Zealand shot 302 in 1977, he had missed the cut here in 1975.

How New Zealand fares in golf's tenth world amateur team championship depends on how newcomers Peter Burney and Alex Bonnington perform. McDougall and Clarke were expected to in the firing line for top individual honors.

McDougall now a veteran of seven Eisenhower's and Clarke a member of two previous teams are in peak form and both have finished in the top 10 in previous world championships. Appropriately, Clarke, won the Peter Stuyvesant Cup a fortnight ago against New Zealand's best amateurs and big Ted was a stroke back equal second.

The tenacious pair then played major roles in New Zealand's defeat of Australia in the Sloan Morpeth Trophy. They teamed for an easy foursomes win, McDougall crushed his opponent in the singles, and Clarke halved his match with a magnificent 25ft putt on the last.

McDougall fired a one-under-par 70 to lead New Zealand to victory over Australia and a Los Angeles club team en route to Portugal. He looks set for big things.

But whether New Zealand improves on its disastrous 15th (its worst placing) in 1974 rests on the shoulders of 22 year old Bonnington and top Aucklander Burney. Bonnington has the power but lacks the precision. Burney has the precision but lacks the power. If they combine their strengths and are not overawed by the occasion, New Zealand could finish in the top five.

New Zealand got off to good start with both McDougall and Clarke firing one-over par 74's and Bonnington and Burney a pair of solid 76s. This placed New Zealand joint 5th with their playing partners for the day the

United States team.

Britain and Ireland were tied with South Africa at the top of the leader board on 219 followed by Sweden and Rhodesia on 223 with New Zealand and the Americans a shot further back on 224. The Australian's were well back on 230. David Suddards from South Africa broke the amateur course record with a 2 under 71.

New Zealand headed into the second round full of confidence however it would be a disastrous day for the Kiwi team. Apart from Clarke who backed up with another 74, Bonnington would be the next best for New Zealand on 79 with McDougall and Burney both shooting 80.

McDougall would comment that he hit only three bad shots which unfortunately lead to three double bogeys and Burney, who made the turn on 1 under par, went to pieces after he three putted from short distance on the 10th green for a double bogey. Bonnington had a bad day on the greens finishing with 39 putts.

Great Britain and Ireland and South Africa were battling it out maintaining their joint position at the top of the leader board. Japan and Australia were the big movers on day two lead by Phil Wood who fired a three under 70. T. M. Chen from Taiwan shot 69, the low round of the day. New Zealand were now well back in eleventh position.

New Zealand bounced back a little on day three lead by McDougall who fired another 74. It could have been much better as he made the turn in three under par however his only bad shot of the day at the 192m par three hole lead to a double bogey 5 and he couldn't convert any of his numerous birdie opportunities on the back nine.

Bonnington and Burney had a pair of respectable 77s with Clarke just off his usual fine touch on the greens shooting 78. Although their three round total of 228 was a five stroke improvement on the previous day they made no progress on the leader board to remain in eleventh position.

Britain and Ireland remained at the top of the leader board with Japan, Australia and the fast moving American's in joint second just two back of the Brits. South Africa slumped on day three to now be well off the pace.

New Zealand totally collapsed in the final round with Clarke (76), McDougall (79), Bonnington (83) and Burney (84) to finish in twelth place. It was a bitterly disappointing end to a tournament that New Zealand went into with such high hopes.

Great Britain and Ireland held onto to win by two from Japan and Australia finished third!

1. Great Britain & Ireland

Ian Hutcheon	73	73	76	71	293
M. J. Kelly	72	76	75	78	301
John Davies	74	75	76	77	302
Steve Martin	75	78	74	76	303
Total	**219**	**224**	**225**	**224**	**892**

2. Japan

Masahiro Kuramoto	75	71	75	73	294
Tetsuo Sakata	76	75	71	83	305
Ginjiro Nakabe	80	74	80	73	307
Micho Mori	76	76	77	78	307
Total	**227**	**220**	**223**	**224**	**894**

3. Australia

Phil Wood	76	70	76	72	294
Tony Gresham	79	78	70	77	304
Colin Kaye	84	72	74	80	310
Chris Bonython	75	79	83	78	315
Total	**230**	**220**	**220**	**227**	**897**

12. New Zealand

Geoff Clarke	74	74	78	76	302
Ted McDougall	74	80	74	79	307
Alex Bonnington	76	79	77	83	315
Peter Burney	76	80	77	84	317
Total	**224**	**233**	**228**	**238**	**923**

For the twenty year period and ten Eisenhower tournaments played from 1958 through to 1976 a total of thirteen players represented New Zealand at the Eisenhower. The New Zealand team's best results were a second in Madrid in 1970 and a third in Rome in 1964.

Their best opportunity for victory was perhaps the very first one when they held a three stroke lead going into the final round. They also had a very good opportunity in Rome when they finished just five behind the winning Great Britain and Ireland team.

The best individual performances are reflected in the table below in the form of notional A and B teams. Sir Bob Charles heads up the A team with top ten individual finishes at both St Andrews and Merion.

McDougall and Murray had remarkably similar results in the seven Eisenhower tournaments they each played in with McDougall having top ten results in Rome and Madrid whilst Murray had top ten results in Rome, Melbourne, and Argentina however I give the second spot to McDougall for his efforts at St Andrews in 1958 when he shot that 72 in the third round and was instrumental in putting New Zealand into the lead. He then backed this up with 75 in the final round.

Clarke rounds out the A team with his performance in Madrid and, whilst outside this period, he had a third place finish in Fiji in 1978.

Stuart Jones heads up the B team. His first five campaigns were disappointing by his standards and didn't come anywhere near close to reflecting his form back home. Ironically his best performance would happen in his last Eisenhower where he had his only top ten finish in Argentina.

Walter Godfrey and Ross Newdick both finished eleventh equal in Japan and had Godfrey not had an 80 in the second round he surely would have finished in the top five.

Bruce Stevens rounds out the B team ahead of John Durry. Stevens finished ahead of Durry in both Mexico and Melbourne and all his eight rounds counted for the team.

John Durry played in four Eisenhower tournaments and failed to break 75 in any of his sixteen rounds. He did however make a significant contribution to New Zealand finishing third in Rome with a final round 75 in difficult weather conditions.

Mike Nicholson and Richard Coombes were very unlucky to make their debuts on the "teeth of the dog" in the Dominican Republic. This was a golf course like no other that the New Zealand team had experienced before and none of the four players would cover themselves in glory here.

Alex Bonnington and Peter Burney, despite a good build up to the Eisenhower in 1976 and also making their debuts, would struggle on the very demanding Penina layout.

All Star A TEAM	Very Good B TEAM
Sir Bob Charles (58,60)	Stuart Jones (58,60,62,64,66,70,72)
Ted McDougall (58,64,68,70,72,74,76)	Walter Godfrey (60,62)
Ross Murray (62,64,66,68,70,72,74)	Ross Newdick (60,62)
Geoff Clarke (70,72,76,78,80)	Bruce Stevens (66,68)

The 1976 Eisenhower would be McDougall's last. He hadn't achieved his ultimate goal of being in a winning Eisenhower team however there had been many successes and friendships made along the way.

Ted would be the last of the 'big four' of New Zealand amateur golf to retire from international play and Geoff Clarke would now play the role that Stuart Jones had played back in 1958 in transitioning from the old guard to the new breed of emerging talent that would take New Zealand amateur golf forward into a new era.

An 18 year old by the name of Frank Nobilo would win the 1978 New Zealand Amateur Championship.

12 RETIREMENT AND THE COMEBACK

In November 1976 the now 65 year old Sam Snead embarked on a twelve day tour of New Zealand including playing in the Otago Charity Classic in Dunedin.

Also on the itinerary was an exhibition match played at the Miramar Golf Club where he partnered Southland's Robyn Low in a four ball best-ball exhibition match against Ted McDougall and Sue Bishop of Canterbury.

They encountered typically windy conditions and although aged 65, Snead with his rhythmical swing, out drove McDougall into the wind with his low boring two wood. When the scores were tallied up however it was McDougall with 75 against Snead's 76.

McDougall was then invited to caddy for Snead in a $1,000 winner take-all match against the Aussie Kel Nagle at Springfield, Rotorua.

McDougall arrived the day before the match and meticulously paced out the yardage of the course. This was a match Snead made clear from the outset he did not want to lose. Torrential rain overnight and early morning had rendered the course almost unplayable.

Thankfully the heavens cleared however a major lake had developed in front of the first green made the first hole temporarily unplayable. The decision was made start the match from the eighth tee, which was located near the club house, with the hope things would have dried out on the first by the time they reached the first hole.

The first hole, being the 8th on the score card, was halved in regulation 4s. The 9th, a long par three, would set the tone for the relationship between Snead and his caddy McDougall. It measures 220 yards however plays slightly down-hill.

McDougall wanted Snead to hit a 4-iron however Snead insisted on a 2-iron and subsequently hit the ball through the back of the green into deep rough. Fortunately Snead hit a great recovery shot and holed his eight-footer for another half.

The match continued with no more than a one hole advantage to either player and the match was indeed all-square when they stood on the tee of the par three 12th, their fifth hole. The pin was back left on this two tiered green.

Over the back of the green was a steep bank which meant certain bogey. Left and right were also not great options. McDougall suggested six iron to this medium length hole playing 176 yards to ensure there wasn't any possibility of Snead going over the back of the green. Snead wanted to hit five iron.

The relationship between McDougall and Snead had been a bit tetchy to say the least up till this point however on this occasion Snead took McDougall's advice and hit the six iron. His back foot appeared to slip slightly just before impact in the slippery conditions. He mishit his shot and to his consternation the ball finished on the bottom tier some 40-feet below the hole.

Snead was none too happy and proceeded to pace out the hole and angrily suggested to McDougall he was 10 yards out with his yardage. Snead putted up to about eight feet short of the hole and then to McDougall's relief he holed the 8-footer to halve the hole for the match to remain all-square.

Snead however continued on with his displeasure with McDougall and there were further words exchanged as they headed to the next tee. McDougall was now at breaking point and offered Snead the option of one of the many golf officials in attendance to carry his bag for the remainder of the match.

At this point Snead changed his tune and put his arm around McDougall and said "*everything is going to be alright Ted*".

The match was still all-square when they stood on the tee at the long dog-leg left par five sixth hole (their 17th). There was no chance Nagle could reach in two however with a perfectly struck tee shot with a nice draw on it and a rifled three wood Snead did just that to set up a win and head to the seventh tee (their 18th) 1up with one to go.

Their last hole was also a par 5 but slightly shorter than the previous hole. Snead could reach this comfortably in two however it would be a stretch for Nagle to reach in two.

When Snead skied his drive McDougall immediately knew there was no chance he could reach in two and with Nagle's renowned short game it was game on. Nagle was short of the green in two about thirty yards slightly right of the green. Snead had come up about twenty yards short.

When Nagle pitched to within an inch of the pin Snead was heard to mutter under his breadth "*I knew the bastard was going to do that*". Snead then proceeded to chip to about three feet from the hole with a severe left to right breaking putt remaining to close out victory.

McDougall couldn't bear to watch however it was the crowds' rapturous reaction to Snead holing his putt confirming Snead had just side-saddled Nagle off the course!

Nagle, however, had the earlier satisfaction of winning the Otago Charity Classic played at St Clair with a score of 274. Snead after a promising 69 in the pro-am finished 23rd equal on a score of 290.

It is now 1977 and McDougall was approaching his 40th birthday. Golf had essentially been the focal point of his life for the past 30 years or more since he started out as a caddy at Pitlochry when he was eight years old.

It was time for a change. His family were growing up fast and his wife Leonie had in essence brought the children up. He successfully applied for the position of Secretary/Manager at the Peninsula Golf Club, Orewa being a 40 minute drive north of Auckland. This would prove to be a good career move.

It meant however he could no longer play representative golf as the role involved some weekend work and he made the decision to retire from competitive golf, however not long before moving north he managed to retain his North Island Stroke Play title in Gisborne where he shared the title with Mike Nicholson.

Results: 1977 North Island Stroke Play - Gisborne Park

1=	**Ted McDougall (Tokoroa)**	**73**	**71**	**69**	**77**	**290**
1=	Mike Nicholson (Whakatane)	69	76	72	73	290
3	Sloan Morpeth (Huntly)	74	74	71	73	292
4=	Rodney Barltrop (Miramar)					294
4=	Mike Barltrop (Fielding)					294

South Island Champs (Balmacewen)

1	Geoff Clarke (St. Clair)	70	71	71	71	283
2	Joe Whittaker (Otago)	70	74	72	77	293
3	Bruce Taylor (Russley)	74	77	74	71	296
4	John Sanders (Otago)					297
5	Ron Johnston (St Clair)					299

When 1982 arrived five years later the New Zealand Amateur was due to be played at Hokowhitu. This had been the venue for Ted's two amateur titles in 1957 and 1970. He decided to take annual leave and entered to take a trip down memory lane.

He paired up with the 1976 and 1977 amateur champion Terry Pulman who had been controversially dropped for the international match against Australia. They combined beautifully to take out the foursomes title. The foursomes are played the day before the qualifying rounds of the match play. Their rounds of 73 and an impressive 4 under 68 in the afternoon gave them a five stroke victory over Taylor & Gaskin and the Australian pairing of Moore & Mackay.

In the two qualifying rounds McDougall was paired with 17-year-old Grant Waite who was the current Australian junior champion. The journalist Graham Skellern recorded McDougall's comments on playing with Waite - *"Yes, he impresses me very much. I admired his natural ability. He gets up and hits the ball very aggressively without forcing it. Grant has got all the length he needs….. I'm a great believer in natural ability carrying you through for years and years"*

They both qualified comfortably in the middle of the 64 qualifiers for the match play. Colin Taylor top qualified with a very impressive 137 being seven stokes clear of his nearest rivals.

McDougall was drawn to play the highly ranked Australian Ossie Moore in the first round of match play. Ted looked to be in control of the match when he was two up after halving the 14th in birdies however Moore birdied three of the last four holes including a crucial one on the last to take out the match 1up.

During the tournament McDougall had struck up a friendship with the talented Ian Peters who at the age of 16 finished the fourth best international at the Junior Masters in the United States. He was now in his early 20s and had just recently returned from a seven month suspension he had received for bad behavior in a major national tournament.

Ian had won his first round without a caddy and McDougall offered his services to caddy which Ian gratefully accepted. It would prove to be a fruitful relationship and as irony would have it McDougall would help Peters plot Ossie Moore's downfall in the final. Ian Peters was the 1982 NZ Amateur Champion.

At the end of 1982 Ted resigned from his role at the Peninsula Golf Club to work in Branch Services at Broadbank's head office in Auckland. This new role would allow Ted to return to playing competitive golf and he held ambitions of playing for Auckland again.

The NZ Amateur in1983 was to be played at one of McDougall's favorite golf courses, the McKenzie designed Titirangi course in west Auckland. Terry Pulman and McDougall again paired up and took out the foursome's title for the second successive year.

The qualifying rounds this particular year were to be played over four rounds with only 32 players to reach the match play stage. Ted had four solid rounds in the mid-70s to qualify 19th equal for the match play. Terry Cochrane was the form player in New Zealand at this time and top qualified with 282.

As the tournament progressed McDougall really hit his straps in the early rounds of the match play with three comfortable wins to set up an intriguing match against Cochrane in the semi-final. In the 36-hole semi-final McDougall made seven birdies to defeat Cochrane 2 and 1 and progress to the final which would be against his old Waikato team mate Colin Taylor.

Taylor was now a regular member of the New Zealand team and had played in the previous two Eisenhower tournaments. He had agonizingly lost to Paul Hartstone on the 38th in the final of the 1980 Amateur after being 4up with four to play.

The headline in the paper on Monday morning would be -**Birdie Burst Sealed Colin's Win** by J. A. Gasparich. -*Five birdies on the trot laid the foundation for 33-year old Taupiri farmer Colin Taylor to beat Ted McDougall 2 and 1 to become the amateur champion of New Zealand at Titirangi yesterday.*

Taylor who had been three down with three to play in the morning finished with a flourish with three consecutive birdies and then proceeded to birdie the first two holes in the afternoon and when McDougall bogeyed the third in the afternoon Taylor had gone from three down to three up in the space of six holes.

McDougall pushed Talyor hard all the way to the finish however Taylor responded to everything McDougall threw at him and he deservedly held on for a 2 and 1 win.

Following the Amateur the two main trial events used as selection for the Auckland team were the Stewart Gold Cup, always played on the Grange course, and the Auckland Stroke Play which was moved around the Auckland region. McDougall would take out his fourth Stewart Gold Cup, a tournament he had previously won as a youngster in 1956-57-58, finishing three ahead of Terry Cochrane.

Results: 1983 Stewart Gold Cup - Grange Golf Club

1	**E. McDougall**	**78**	**73**	**71**	**72**	**294**
2	T. Cochrane	73	75	75	74	297
3=	B. Soland	78	73	71	76	298
3=	G. Goldfinch	74	76	70	78	298
5	S. Partridge	69	78	76	78	301
6	T. Morrin	72	73	81	76	302
7=	P. Shadlock	75	81	74	75	305
7=	T. Webber	77	73	74	81	305
7=	G. Dyer	78	74	74	79	305
10	R. Peploe	76	78	74	78	306

The Auckland stroke play was played on his home track at Peninsula where he finished second two strokes behind the promising 18-year-old Glen Goldfinch. McDougall was duly named in the Auckland team and after warm up representative matches against Wellington and Waikato was named number three for the Auckland team to play in the interprovincial tournament to be played at St Andrews in Hamilton.

The Auckland team of Barltrop, Cochrane, McDougall, Goldfinch and Partridge were in good form and after five rounds were undefeated with five straight wins. The Canterbury team of Paterson, Lapsley, M. Street, Sanders and Minifie were also in good form with five straight wins.

The interprovincial tournament would be determined by the outcome of the match between Canterbury and Auckland on the morning of the final day. Canterbury prevailed over Auckland and made no mistakes in the afternoon to win the Government Life sponsored event convincingly.

Bob Schumacher would write in The Press:

It was Paterson who really shook Auckland's confidence - Barltrop could not believe he was 6 down after 10 holes for he was only one over par

Lapsley, calculating and confident as always, comfortably overcame international team-mate Terry Cochrane.

Minifie, the fragile-built Waitikiri player, showed what a fine player he is under pressure… judged his putt to perfection on the tricky eighteenth green to get his par and win the hole when Partridge three putted.

Street tried hard and took Glen Goldfinch, who putted excellently, to the last hole before succumbing.

Sanders rifled in deadly approach shots on 15, 16, and 17 to quash the last resistance from McDougall.

Mr. Barry Cotton, the nonplaying Canterbury captain, was a proud man and quite moved when Canterbury sealed its win against Auckland.

In 1984 McDougall was appointed branch manager for Broadbank in Whangarei, Northland. During his brief two year stay here he represented Northland at No. 2 behind Kevin Billington in the Government Life sponsored interprovincial tournament in New Plymouth and again at Invercargill in 1985.

Then in 1985 at the age of 47 he played in his last New Zealand Amateur at Mt Maunganui. He qualified in the top 32 but lost in the first round against Ray Picker of Australia. The first round losers and the second- group of 32 qualifiers then play a separate match play event for the ' NZ Plate'. McDougall won through to the final and beat Bill Sipson 2up. Many a top player has won this event!

In 1986 McDougall returned to Auckland and back into Head Office for Broadbank. He decided he wanted to get into good physical condition in an effort to once again play for Auckland. He joined up with Jim Blair, a well-known fitness guru, at the Institute of Sport in Auckland and within four months they had got his weight down from 19st 13lb to under 18 stone with a target to get down to 16 and a half stone.

This fitness regime brought instant results when he blitzed the field by nine strokes to win his first Auckland Stroke Play title at the age of 49.

Results: 1986 Auckland Stroke Play - Maungakiekie Golf Club

1	**E. McDougall**	67	73	70	70	280
2=	M. Barltrop	69	76	67	77	289
2=	T. Cochrane	76	71	72	70	289
4	P. Aickin	70	73	71	76	290
5	P. Hanish	73	76	70	72	291
6	G. Steigmeier	78	74	67	73	292
7=	K. Hankin	73	69	73	78	293
7=	G. Hattaway	70	73	71	79	293
9	J. Oliver	70	75	76	73	294
10	G. Stephens	73	76	72	74	295

The significance of this performance cannot be overstated as the field included some of the best amateurs in the country at the time including Michael Barltrop, Terry Cochrane and Philip Aickin. These players had been the back bone of New Zealand representative teams throughout the early and mid -1980s.

In his report on the event the journalist Brian Doherty would write -*"It was a flashback to the past when McDougall was at the height of his considerable powers. Back came the long driving - the 389-metre fourth and number 1 stroke hole was nothing but a nine-iron second for McDougall when most of the players would have been happy to hit seven iron - and the delicate shot making was there too"*.

McDougall backed this up by making the semi-finals of the Auckland match play before going down to Philip Aickin. Ted was subsequently named number five for this very formidable looking Auckland team.

In a warm up match to the interprovincial tournament Auckland beat Waikato 15.5 to 4.5 at the Grange. The highlight of this event was the match between the 15-year-old Philip Tataurangi and the 49 year old Ted McDougall. Tataurangi was 2up after a birdie on the 14th but, as J. A. Gasparich would write, -*he then stood by mesmerized as McDougall won the 16th*

17th, and 18ᵗʰ to take the match 1up.

The format for the Government Life Men's Interprovincial Tournament was now broken into to two groups of seven teams with the top two from each group playing off in a semi-final and final.

Auckland were convincing winners of their group and met Waikato in the final. Auckland looked to be in control of the final but the tide turned when McDougall, who was four up with eight to play, lost 1-down to John Gatley.

David Jackson completed the come back when he holed a 20-foot put on the final green against Philip Aickin that denied Auckland a play-off. Waikato had won 3-2. The Waikato No. 3 Alan Smith was named player of the tournament.

It was a very disconsolate McDougall at the end of his match against Gatley as the realization sunk in that a grand opportunity had been missed to be part of a record breaking sixth winning team.

However it didn't take long for McDougall to bounce back from this disappointment. The Omanu Classic is a major attraction for many of New Zealand's leading amateurs. It is played in the idyllic Bay of Plenty at Mt. Maunganui on the Omanu links.

This particular year it also attracted the highly rated Australian Ray Picker who would ultimately run away from the field with a final round 67. McDougall however was almost as equally impressive.

Results: Omanu Classic - December 1986.

1	R. Picker (Cowra, NSW)	73	69	71	67	280
2	O. Kendall (Mt Maunganui)	72	68	71	74	285
3	**E. McDougall (Peninsula)**	**72**	**69**	**74**	**71**	**286**
4=	A. Smith (Hamilton)	69	74	74	71	288
4=	E. Boult (Blenheim)	72	73	71	72	288

6=	P. Yelavich (Mt Maunganui)	73	71	72	74	290
6=	A. Methven (RNZAF Whenuapai)	75	72	71	72	290
6=	D. Cooke (Omanu)	74	71	74	71	290
6=	M. Nicholson (Tauranga)	75	72	74	69	290
10=	G. Amos (Omanu)	69	71	76	75	291
10=	P. Aickin (Whitford Park)	70	74	72	75	291
12=	J. Williamson (Christchurch)	72	73	73	74	292
12=	R. Burney (Manukau)	70	79	70	73	292
14=	P. Mosley (North Shore)	75	74	72	72	293
14=	B. Paterson (Coringa)	72	75	71	75	293
14=	D. Jackson (Putaruru)	73	75	72	73	293

Since coming out of retirement in 1982 McDougall had accomplished some very impressive results and since joining up with Jim Blair and the Auckland Institute of Sport he had now regained some of his immense strength which had always been a feature of his game.

He was now at the peak of his comeback and his stroke play results were at a level that was at least equal to the New Zealand team representatives who competed at the 1986 Eisenhower being Michael Barltrop, Philip Aickin, Glen Goldfinch and Brent Paterson.

During his comeback McDougall had indicated to the NZ-selectors, via the press, that he was once again available for selection for the national team. The response was a deafening silence.

The Auckland Anniversary tournament is played in January every year on the Akarana golf course and is the first of the three major Auckland stroke play events held each year, the others being the Stewart Gold Cup and the Auckland Stroke Play.

Not too far off his 50th birthday Ted won this event for the first time by beating Phil Aickin in a playoff.

Results: 1987 Auckland Anniversary Tournament - Akarana Golf Club

1	**E. McDougall**	**71**	**75**	**75**	**221**
2	P. Aickin	73	73	75	221
3	B. Smith	72	74	76	222
4=	T. Cochrane	77	71	76	224
4=	G. Todd	76	73	75	224
4=	K. Hankin	82	72	70	224
7=	R. McBride	77	73	76	226
7=	D. McDougall	78	74	74	226
7=	M. Leitch	79	73	74	226
10	V. Pirihi	74	76	77	227

McDougall won play-off: 4-5

This event was the main trial for selection of the Auckland team to contest the South Invitational tournament. McDougall was duly selected.

He was instrumental in Auckland winning the Southland invitational teams' stroke play event played in March 1987. The Invitational includes five players from each province in New Zealand and has an Eisenhower format where the four best rounds of each team are totaled for each round.

Auckland were well back in fourth equal place at the half way mark. Auckland's two national representative players, Barltrop and Aickin, were away in Australia playing in the Riversdale Cup and McDougall was made captain of a virtual Auckland 'B' team. He rallied the troops on Sunday and when he fired 69 and 70 himself Auckland had staged a remarkable comeback to edge Canterbury and take the title by a massive fourteen strokes.

Ted had a four round total of 295 to finish three behind Glen Goldfinch

(Auckland) and Fred Poskitt (Canterbury). On 294 was Stephen Partridge (Auckland) and Terry Cochrane (Auckland) also had 295. This was Auckland's first win in this event since 1981.

George Lasker (Waikato) and Fred Poskitt had the low round of 68 for the tournament.

Results;

1. Auckland 1169

2. Canterbury 1183

3. Wellington 1195

After the disappointment at Hokowhitu the previous year Ted still held ambitions of playing one more interprovincial and he put in consistent performances at the Stewart Gold Cup and Auckland Stroke Play by finishing equal 4th in each event however when he was selected at number six to play against Northland the omens were not looking good to make the five man team for the interprovincial.

He was now 50 years of age and the selectors were concerned about his fitness levels for the week-long event despite the fact he was still attending the gym and in reasonably good shape. Needless to say he wasn't selected and was now relegated to playing in the masters event for the over 40s.

It was 1957 all over again where he had won all and sundry in Auckland but was incontinently dropped from the Freyberg Rose Bowl team (now the Government Life interprovincial tourney).

Ted graciously accepted his demotion to the masters team and he led Auckland to two victories at Templeton in Christchurch and Akarana in Auckland. The Auckland team dominated at Akarana when they won 30.5 out of a possible 35 individual matches culminating in a 5-0 drubbing over Canterbury in the final round. This would be McDougall's last representative match.

There was an interesting side line story during the tourney written by J. A GASPARICH under the headline;

Southern southpaw topples McDougall

Dusty Miller, a southpaw from the Greenacres club in Invercargill, realized a personal ambition when he beat the Auckland No 1, Ted McDougall, in the second round of the Freyberg Masters tournament at Akarana yesterday.

The 44-year old Miller, a Southland representative in 1980 when the Freyberg Rose Bowl was the Premier interprovincial tournament, came to Akarana with the prime purpose of beating former New Zealand representatives Paul Hartstone and McDougall.

In Monday's opener, Miller realized part of that dream, halving his match with Hartstone. Yesterday he went a step better hustling McDougall off the course 4 and 3.

Miller was still in top form in the afternoon, beating Bob Bailey (Hawkes Bay), who incidentally had also halved with Hartstone, 2up.

"I planned this tournament far ahead," said Miller. "I spent three months doing gym work, enjoyed it, and it has done the world of good for me."

While Miller was three up with four to play against Hartstone and then let it slip away he was in a different frame of mind against McDougall.

He made birdie on three of the par three holes, finished with birdie on three of the last four holes. He confessed the win equaled his previous big success, winning the 1990 national left-handed championship.

Congratulations Dusty, you just beat *The Greatest Amateur in the World*.

At the age of 54 the 1991 New Zealand senior title for golfers aged 50 and over would be Ted's last significant act in his adventurous and mostly enjoyable golfing career.

He won by nine strokes on the Akarana course in Auckland on a score of 222 for the 54-hole event.

Results: 1991 New Zealand Seniors - Akarana Golf Club

1	**E. McDougall**	**222**
2=	W. Sherrin	231

2=	B. Olgilvy	231
4	V. Pirihi	232
5	C. Jacobson	233

In January the following year Ted again required back surgery in a five hour operation to relieve pressure on his lower back. The surgeon chiseled out his spinal column, removing quite a bit of bone to free up nerves. Although the procedure was successful this would be the start of a rapid decline in his physical capability and lead to a premature diminished golfing prowess.

I leave the final words to Winston Hooper taken from the *Waikato Golf Association Celebrates its first 50 years 1947-1997* booklet that aptly and succinctly describes McDougall's personality and also reflects on his achievements of the past 40 years;

His rhythmical and powerful swing regularly pumped 280 yard plus drives and when in the mood the 300 yard plus par four greens were at his mercy. In 1968 at Ngamotu he drove to the edge of the 365 yard 13th and then holed his chip for an eagle two. In spite of his back, and then hip problems which meant hospital stays in the mid-1960s and early 1970s, McDougall wowed overseas journalists. After his Spain success they said his driving was the most brutally effective in the amateur ranks, his superbly struck irons would bring huge pay cheques on the US tour, his short game was like a loving caress with such soft hands, his recovery work, when needed, masterly, and for a big man he had a silken touch on the greens. Back home the media labelled him - 'The One-ton wonder from Tokoroa', and so on. He was happiest when he could relax with his Waikato colleagues around him. He was a great believer in team spirit. Perhaps his desire for fun got him offside from time to time, but there was no questioning his dedication to the cause. When he played to his potential, daylight was second.

THE END

Edward John (Ted) McDougall (Born 1937 Dundee, Scotland)- Mother-Jane Hendry, (Born 1899, Monifieth)

Pitlochry High School Champion 1950, 1951

Scottish Midland Boys Champion 1951

New Zealand Amateur Champion 1957, 1970

Runner-up NZ Amateur 1964, 1969, 1983

Leading Amateur NZ Open 1967, 1970

Leading Qualifier NZ Amateur 1969, 1970

NZ Foursomes Champion 1957, 1970, 1982, 1983

North Island Stroke Play Champion 1964, 1968, 1976, 1977

North Island versus South Island (Sponsored by Peter Stuyvesant)- Individual Champion 1975

Stewart Gold Cup Champion 1956, 1957, 1958, 1983

Auckland Stroke Play Champion 1986

Auckland Match Play Champion 1962

Auckland Anniversary Tournament Champion 1987

Northland Match Play Champion 1957, 1982

Waikato Stroke Play Champion 1965, 1969, 1970, 1976, 1977

New Zealand Senior Champion 1991

NZ Representative

- Sloan Morpeth Trophy v Australia 1964, 1965, 1969, 1976
- Commonwealth Tournament 1975 South Africa
- Colombian International 1975
- Eisenhower Trophy 1958, 1964 (NZ 3RD), 1968, 1970 (NZ 2ND), 1972, 1974, 1976

Interprovincial (Freyberg Rose Bowl)-member of the following winning teams:

- Auckland 1958
- Waikato 1968, 1971, 1972, 1974

Southland Invitational-member of the following winning team:

- Auckland 1987

Club Champion

- Pukekohe Golf Club 1956, 1957
- Muriwai Golf Club 1963
- Tokoroa Golf Club 1965, 1967, 1968, 1974, 1975
- Peninsula Golf Club 1979, 1980, 1981, 1987, 1988, 1989, 1992, 1993

Professional Tournaments

- Tauranga Invitational 1957 (Won as an amateur), 1959
- New Plymouth Golf Club Sponsored Tournament 1959
- Auckland Open 1959

E. J. McDougall - International Match Play Record

Sloan Morpeth Trophy played for against Australia				
Year & Venue	**Foursomes**	**Result**	**Singles**	**Result**
1964 Sydney (Pennant Hills)	*McDougall & Durry v Baker & Billings*	*Loss 2&1*	*Versus Phillip Billings*	*All Square*
1965 Christchurch (Shirley Links)	*McDougall & Durry v Billings & Donohoe*	*Win 2&1*	*Versus Phillip Billings*	*Win 4&3*
1969 Adelaide (Grange)	*McDougall & Brown v Toogood & MacKay*	*Win 7&5*	*Versus Sonny MacKay*	*Win 2up*
1976 Auckland (Muriwai)	*McDougall & Clarke v Kaye & Bonython*	*Win 4&3*	*Versus Chris Bonython*	*Win 5&4*
Commonwealth Tournament 1975 (Royal Durban South Africa)				
Versus Britain	*McDougall & Reese v Greig & McGregor*	*Win 4&3*	*Versus David Greig*	*Win 3&2*
Versus South Africa	*McDougall & Reese v Todt & Dreyer*	*Loss 2&1*	*Versus Peter Todt*	*Win 4&3*
Versus Canada	*McDougall & Reese v Nelford & Fergusson*	*Loss 3&2*	*Versus Ces Furguson*	*Loss 1 Down*
Summary	**Foursomes**	**4 Wins - 3 Losses**	**Singles**	**5 ½ Wins - 1 ½ Losses**

Head to Head with the 'Emperor' of New Zealand Golf - Stuart Jones

Stuart Jones may have lauded it over most golfers in New Zealand however the *Barron of Bridge Par* certainly didn't laud it over the *Terror from Tokoroa*.

Match	Year	Event	Venue	McDougall	Jones
1	1957	NZ Amateur	Hokowhitu	3 and 2	
2	1958	Freyberg	Nelson	1 up	
3	1964	Final - NZ Amateur	Hamilton		37th
4	1965	Freyberg	Waitikiri	5 and 4	
5	1965	Waikato v Hawkes Bay	Taupo		3 and 2
6	1968	Freyberg	New Plymouth	All Square	All Square
7	1968	Waikato v Hawkes Bay	Cambridge	1 up	
8	1969	Freyberg	The Hutt	2 and 1	
9	1969	Waikato v Hawkes Bay	Napier		5 and 4
10	1970	Waikato v Hawkes Bay	Tokoroa	3 and 2	
11	1971	Waikato v Hawkes Bay	Maranui	2 and 1	
12	1974	NZ Amateur	Manukau	3 and 2	
Total				8.5	3.5

Head to Head with Sir Michael Bonallack

McDougall and Bonallack, perhaps the finest amateur of his generation, each played in seven Eisenhower tournaments between 1958 and 1976. They each participated at the same Eisenhower tournament on four occasions. (See comparison below)

Sir Michael Bonallack (Great Britain and Ireland)

Year	Venue	Round 1	Round 2	Round 3	Round 4	72 Hole
1964	Rome	80	76	77	78	311
1968	Melbourne	72	72	66	76	286
1970	Madrid	75	74	75	75	299
1972	Buenos Aires	71	73	75	76	295
Total						1191
Average						74.44

Ted McDougall (New Zealand)

Year	Venue	Round 1	Round 2	Round 3	Round 4	72 Hole
1964	Rome	72	76	77	74	299
1968	Melbourne	75	75	77	75	302
1970	Madrid	72	73	73	70	288
1972	Buenos Aires	76	78	72	72	298
Total						1187
Average						74.19

NOTABLE EISENHOWER PLAYERS - (World Amateur Team Championships)

Below is my assessment of the leading 21 players to have played between the dates of 1958 through to 1976. To qualify for this list each player must have played in at least three Eisenhower tournaments. This eliminates the many quality players who played in either one or two events prior to turning professional and leaves in essentially the players who had amateur careers.

All the courses they played on during this period were of a high standard and very challenging and often played in inclement weather conditions. A four round total of under 300 was a fine achievement. A four round total of under 290 was an exceptional achievement hence any player who had a total score of under 290 automatically made the top 10.

1) Marvin Giles III - United States of America (68,70,72)
  a. Tied 1ST individual in Melbourne 1968, **score 286.**
  b. Finished 7th individual in Madrid 1970, **score 289.**
  c. Finished 2nd equal individual in Buenos Aires 1972, **score 287.**

2) Ronald D.B.M Shade - Great Britain & Ireland (62,64,66,68)
  a. Finished 5th individual in Japan 1962.
  b. Leading individual in Mexico 1966, **score 283.**
  c. Finished 9th individual in Melbourne 1968.

3) William Hyndman III - United States of America (58,60)
  a. William Hyndman III is the one exception to my rule of playing in three Eisenhower's to qualify for my list as his international amateur career started later in life and his performance in the two he played were outstanding.
  b. Finished tied 1st individual at St Andrews 1958.
  c. Finished 4th individual at Merion 1960, **score 287.**

4) Deane Beman - United States of America (60,62,64,66)
  a. Finished 2nd individual at Merion, 1960, **score 282.**
  b. Finished 3rd individual in Japan, 1962, **score 286.**
  c. Finished 4th individual in Mexico 1966.

5) Anthony Gresham - Australia (68,70,72,74,76,78,80)
  a. Finished 4th individual in Madrid 1970, **score 287.**
  b. Leading individual in Buenos Aires 1972, **score 285.**

6) Edward (Ted) McDougall - New Zealand (58,64,68,70,72,74,76)
  a. Finished 7th individual in Rome in 1964.
  b. Finished 6th individual in Madrid 1970, **score 288.**

7) Michael Bonallack - Great Britain & Ireland (60,62,64,66,68,70,72,)

    a. Finished 8th individual in Japan 1962.

    b. Tied 1st best individual in Melbourne 1968, **score 286.**

    c. Finished 9th= in Buenos Aires 1972.

8) *Gary Cowan - Canada (60,62,64,66,68,70,78)*

    a. Leading individual in Japan 1960, **score 280.**

    b. Finished 7th individual in Melbourne 1968.

9) *Juan Estrada - Mexico (60,62,64,66,68)*

    a. Finished 8th individual at Merion 1960.

    b. Finished 4th individual in Japan 1962, **score 287**

10) *Ian Hutcheon - Great Britain & Ireland (74,76,80)*

    a. Tied 1st individual at Penina 1976.

11) *Nick Weslock - Canada (62,64,66,72)*

12) *Kevin Donohoe - Australia (62,66,68,70)*

13) *Ross Murray - New Zealand (62,64,66,68,70,72,74)*

14) *Phillip Billings - Australia (62,64,66)*

15) *Chien Chin Chen - China (60,62,64,66,68,70,72,)*

16) *Geoff Clarke - New Zealand (70,72,76,78,80)*

17) *David Symons - South Africa (66,68,70)*

18) *Ginjiro Nakabe - Japan (62,66,68,74,76,78)*

19) *Jaime Gonzalez - Brazil (70,72,74)*

20) *Robert Wylie - Canada (60,62,68,84)*

21) *Keith Alexander - Canada (60,66,70,72)*

Top 10 Players in the North Island v South Island tournament.

1975 Russley Par 219		1976 Titirangi Par 216		1977 Russley Par 73		1978 Manukau Par 213	
E. J. McDougall	209	G. E Clarke	213	P. E. Hartstone	70	Peter Burney	216
A. W. Bonnington	215	E. J. McDougall	214	M. E. Barltrop	72	Geoff Saunders	216
S. F. Reese	218	P. A. Reid	214	R. J. Johnston	73	Paul Hartstone	218
P. E. Hartstone	219	P. A. Maude	215	S. J. Barron	73	Michael Barltrop	218
P. K. Creighton	219	R. C. Murray	215	M. J. Bartlett	74	Jim Lapsley	219
R. M. Barltrop	220	N. A. L. Gaskin	220	I. A. Peters	74	Kim McDonald	220
O. J. Kendall	221	K. R. Hankin	220	T. R. Pulman	74	Frank Nobilo	221
G. E. Clarke	221	C. J. Hoole	220	N. A. L. Gaskin	75	Peter Creighton	225
R. Barker	222	J. B. Sanders	220	K. L. Martin	75	Phil Reid	225
P. F. Garner	222	C. E. Alldred	221	P. W. Mosley	75	P.Burney M.Nicholson R. Johnston J. B. Sanders	226

In 1977 snow forced the tourney to be reduced to 18 holes.

Players who have played 100 or more Inter-Provincial games and their percentage win record.

Stuart Jones	176	1	Peter Creighton	71.3%
Charlie Alexander	163	2	Stuart Jones	70.7%
Colin Taylor	149	3	Ross Murray	68.8%
John Durry	149	4	Ted McDougall	64.9%
Rodney Barltrop	148	5	John Sanders	64.5%
Ross Murray	148	6	Ian McDonald	61.6%
Jim Lapsley	140	7	John Durry	60.9%
Kevin Downie	136	8	Rodney Barltrop	60.5%
Paul Adams	136	9	Kevin Billington	59.3%
Mike Nicholson	130	10	Brent McEwan	59.2%
Ian McDonald	125	11	Ken Hankin	57.5%
Peter Creighton	123	12	Jim Lapsley	56.8%
Ted McDougall	115	13	Neil Gaskin	56.8%
Kevin Billington	113	14	Colin Taylor	56.4%
Neil Gaskin	111	15	Mike Nicholson	53.5%
Ken Hankin	107	16	Paul Adams	49.6%
A. C. Relph	105	17	Kevin Downie	48.5%
Gary Radka	103	18	A. C. Relph	44.2%
Brent McEwan	103	19	Gary Radka	44.2%
P. D. Rouse	101	20	Charlie Alexander	42.6%
John Sanders	100	21	P. D. Rouse	41.6%

ABOUT THE AUTHOR

Golf was all consuming growing up in our family. I first became aware of how good my father was as a golfer when I was about eleven years old. My first vivid recollection was when New Zealand finished second at the 1970 World Amateur Team Championship held in Spain. I would often caddy for my father in tournaments. The family summer vacation was always three weeks spent at Omanu Beach, Mt. Maunganui. The NZPGA during the 1970s alternated between Mt. Maunganui and Tauranga whilst we were on holiday. I would caddy for my father in this event and he would often be paired with some of the best golfers in world golf at that time. When I left high school I attended Otago University and studied accountancy where I was fortunate enough to play several rounds of golf with Greg Turner - when he returned from Oklahoma where he was on a golf scholarship. Greg played in two Eisenhower tournaments before turning professional and he would become a prolific winner on the Australian and European tours. He was New Zealand's most naturally talented and gifted player of my generation. In 1996 I was fortunate enough to compete in the Brabazon Trophy at Royal St. Georges, The St. Andrews Links Trophy at St. Andrews and the British Amateur at Turnberry. I eventually settled in Christchurch, NZ where I experienced the most terrifying events of my life when the September 2010 and February 2011 earthquakes struck Christchurch. My home club, the Christchurch Golf Club, was destroyed in the February earthquake and has only recently been rebuilt. This was the venue for the 1990 Eisenhower where NZ finished second equal. Two years later in 1992 New Zealand would be victorious in Canada. I still live in Christchurch with Isobel and our six year old son Brodie. In 2015 I had a far more memorable experience when I played alongside Dame Laura Davies in the New Zealand Woman's Open pro-am.

Printed in Great Britain
by Amazon